MW01194191

realrecovery

Endorsements for
Real Recovery

If you've ever let a single pound gained ruin your day, this book is for you. If you've ever seen food as your enemy and thinness as your very best friend, this book is for you. If you've looked to programs, websites, apps, or do-better-mantras to help you overcome your battle with an eating disorder only to find yourself stuck in the same destructive patterns, this book is for you. Because all women struggle with disordered eating patterns and all people look to the wrong sources for hope, this book is for all of us. In her raw book *Real Recovery: What Eating Disorder Recovery Actually Looks Like*, Grace points us to the only Source of true hope and lasting change, Jesus and His Word. Let her story inspire you to open your Bible and live a life freer in Christ.

Erin Davis

Bible Teacher, Author of *Graffiti: Learning to See the Art in Ourselves*
Co-author of *Fasting & Feasting: 40 Devotions to Satisfy the Hungry Heart*

This book is an excellent tool for anyone who wants to understand what it is like to walk through and recover from an eating disorder. Grace's openness and authenticity invite the reader to journey with her through the ups and downs of her struggle with anorexia nervosa, guided by the valuable insights of counselors and doctors. Her story will be a blessing to those who are in recovery themselves.

Taylor Eising

Editorial Assistant for *Unlocked* devotional magazine for teens

Grace McCready has created a beautifully authentic book filled with personal insight about her road to recovery from anorexia. Embracing both the myths and reality of her painful journey, Grace shares the bumpy road of fighting to silence her negative self-talk (which she names "Ed" for Eating Disorder) in order to live free in Christ. In *Real Recovery*, Grace sets expectations and provides an honest guidebook for those in recovery and their loved ones.

Cyndie Claypool de Neve

Associate Marriage and Family Therapist

Author of *God-Confident Kids: Helping Your Child Find True Purpose, Passion and Peace*

If you want a peek inside the heart of someone who has walked the difficult journey of an eating disorder, this is the perfect book for you. Grace peeled back the layers of her heart and showed the actual journey one walks while trying to find recovery transparently and authentically. As a counselor myself, I found such truth and power in Grace's writing. I would love to hand this book to clients who are walking their recovery journey so they could have this trusted friend help them see they are not alone. I am so grateful that Grace offered her actual recovery journey for us and the truths that helped her walk free. This book is a treasure for a struggling heart.

Jennifer Hand

Author of *My Yes is on the Table: Moving from Fear to Faith*

Podcaster at Coming Alive Conversations

Executive Director of Coming Alive Ministries

God created our bodies and the food that fills them to reflect His beauty and goodness. And yet, sin and Satan are constantly trying to twist God's design into something poisonous. This is the broken reality of living with an eating disorder, and Grace knows that better than most. Her book offers a raw, starkly honest, and desperately needed glimpse into the dark valley of anorexia, also providing truly helpful advice for those walking the long path of recovery. Her words will encourage, convict, and point you to Jesus every step of the way.

Naomi Vacaro

Author of *Quiet: Creating Grace-Based Rhythms for Spending Time with Jesus*

Founder of the Wholehearted community

realrecovery

What Eating Disorder Recovery Actually Looks Like

GRACE MCCREADY

AMBASSADOR INTERNATIONAL
GREENVILLE, SOUTH CAROLINA & BELFAST, NORTHERN IRELAND

www.ambassador-international.com

Real Recovery
What Eating Disorder Recovery Actually Looks Like
©2022 by Grace McCready
All rights reserved

ISBN: 978-1-64960-209-1
eISBN: 978-1-64960-317-3

Cover Design by Hannah Linder Designs
Interior Typesetting by Dentelle Design
Edited by Katie Cruice Smith

The Holy Bible, English Standard Version. ESV® Text Edition: 2016. Copyright © 2001 by Crossway Bibles, a publishing ministry of Good News Publishers.

Disclaimer: The contents of this book are not a substitute to professional assessment or treatment of mental or emotional disorders. Rather it is a forestep aiding the individual in self-identification of the effects of personal choice in contributing to their present life situation. It assumes that each individual is capable of making life enhancing decisions.

No part of this publication may be reproduced, distributed, or transmitted in any form or by any means, including photocopying, recording, or other electronic or mechanical methods, without the prior written permission of the publisher, except in the case of brief quotations embodied in critical reviews and certain other noncommercial uses permitted by copyright law. For permission requests, contact the publisher using the information below.

AMBASSADOR INTERNATIONAL
Emerald House
411 University Ridge, Suite B14
Greenville, SC 29601
United States
www.ambassador-international.com

AMBASSADOR BOOKS
The Mount
2 Woodstock Link
Belfast, BT6 8DD
Northern Ireland, United Kingdom
www.ambassadormedia.co.uk

The colophon is a trademark of Ambassador, a Christian publishing company.

To the One Who saved me from me—Jesus Christ, my Redeemer and Rescuer.

Table of Contents

Foreword

As Grace's therapist, I had the privilege of walking alongside her during the latter part of her journey through anorexia, so this book is a living testimony to me that with the help of family members, friends, doctors, and counselors, individuals *can* find healing from their eating disorders.

The work that you'll have to do in order to recover won't be easy, as Grace emphasizes throughout this book. Sometimes, you'll feel like you're trudging through wet sand. You won't be able to wave away your struggles with a magic wand. You may not get the happily ever after that you'll so desperately desire. And although your behavior may gradually change like Grace's did, you may still feel the pull of Ed's familiar voice that promises freedom but only keeps you in bondage.

The only way to refute the lies that you're believing about yourself is to do what Grace advises in the pages ahead: replace them with the truth of who you are in Christ. Meditate on them. Breathe them into your soul. Let your Heavenly Father show you that you're loved no matter what size you are.

Sometimes, you'll feel motivated. Other times, you'll feel like you're falling backward and can't stop falling. The pull of Ed's voice will be intense. After all, your identity is at stake. And your identity is at the core of your eating disorder.

Ed wants to keep you from finding your true identity. Your authentic self. The person God designed you to be.

You see, your eating disorder isn't really about food or exercise. It's about all of the moments that you abandon your true identity by following Ed's voice when something difficult happens so that you'll avoid the pain, loneliness, or disconnection that you feel deep down. And guess what? Even after you've put all of your energy into eating less and exercising more, my guess is that you'll still feel empty, alone, and fat.

The truth is that you're looking for something that you believe will fill you—something that'll make you feel happy, secure, adequate, and accepted. In your mind, that something is thinness. But thin is never thin enough, as Grace points out later on.

After working with eating disordered clients for twenty-five years, I have a few insights to share about the realities of eating disorders and recovery.

First, you need to remember that you—and only you—can do the work to recover. That's what Grace did. She was an active participant in her treatment, even when she didn't want to be. She listened to her healthcare team. She challenged her toxic thinking. Most importantly, she started to listen to who God said she was instead of listening to who Ed said she was. And she made progress in her recovery.

Second, you need to have support from committed people who will walk alongside you for the long haul. They should be emotionally attuned and available. They should be patient and listen to you instead of judging you. As you confide in them and as they invest in you, they're planting seeds for growth in your life.

Third, you need to choose words to describe the losses of life that have broken your heart. The pain, suffering, and hopelessness that you have felt and still feel should be processed with a trusted counselor. Denying your pain or burying your pain aren't wise options if you want to really recover from your eating disorder.

Fourth, you need to learn to accept who you are. This may be the hardest thing that you do during your recovery, and it'll take a significant amount of time. Remember that surrender doesn't mean giving up; it means freedom. It's relinquishing the right to have skinniness be the most important thing in your life. As long as you have to be the skinniest girl in the room, Ed will always own you.

Fifth, you need to find your identity in Christ, not in Ed. Jesus said that if you choose to trust Him, He'll meet all of your needs (Phil. 4:10-19). The apostle Peter wrote, "His divine power has granted to us all things that pertain to life and godliness, through the knowledge of him who called us to his own glory and excellence" (2 Peter 1:3). Those words are in cement.

Knowing this, you have to decide if you truly want to recover from your eating disorder. Only you can make that decision. If you choose Ed, you'll spend the rest of your life running on a performance treadmill to try to make yourself okay when the truth is that you already are.

Grace has walked this road before you, and she's giving you a roadmap to follow. Take her hand (and the Savior's hand) and walk into the light.

Rita A. Schulte, LPC

Introduction

I don't know if I should share this secret with you, but before you dive into the first chapter, I think I should tell you that I'm not fully recovered from anorexia—at least not in the sense that you might think.

You might expect that gaining weight is a miniscule concern in my life right now, that food doesn't scare me anymore, and that I work out because I find it enjoyable. Or perhaps you expect that I think that my recovered body feels like a great fit, that I don't hear lies about my body anymore, that I love my body as much as I love anyone else's, or that guys are captivated by my body. Or maybe you expect that my relationship with God is practically perfect, that I no longer care to control anything in my life, or that I'm truly "all better" from anorexia.

None of that is me.

The real me still feels anxious about stepping on the scale, still has fears about the nutrition labels she sees (or can't see), and still is adamant about exercising daily. She still wants to hide the waist that she can't change, still wishes that Satan would leave her alone, still wants the body that her friend has, and still wonders why a guy has never told her that she's beautiful. She still feels like spiritual freedom is abstract, still attempts to control her life and others' lives, and still struggles to call herself "recovered."

All of that is me.

The reason that I tell you so soon that I'm not fully recovered from anorexia—at least not in the sense of forgetful bliss—is that I don't want you to have the wrong idea about this book. This book doesn't have a happily ever after, though many other eating disorder stories, memoirs, and self-help books do. I hope that fact actually makes you feel better so that you won't think that you're abnormal if you never fully recover from your eating disorder in the way that those authors describe recovery.

I may never fully recover from my eating disorder if it means forgetting what a scale, a nutrition label, and a workout are. You may never fully recover that way either. But that *doesn't* mean that you have to stay stuck where you are right now. The goal of this book is to show you that, in reality, recovery from an eating disorder means being able to take one step forward at a time—not necessarily being able to run away at top speed.

I want *you* to know what *I* didn't know when I started recovering from an eating disorder. And if we were to meet in person (which would be pretty amazing), I would want you to see me as someone who's passionate about the truth because that's who I am. I'm passionate about being real in our churches, friendships, and families. I'm also passionate about fighting Satan's lies, which, as I personally discovered, make it very difficult to recover from an eating disorder. Thus, I'm very anti-fakeness and pro-authenticity. Authenticity makes all the difference, especially for individuals who are recovering from an eating disorder.

That's why each chapter is titled with a False Expectation, which you may have gained by hearing or reading about eating disorders in the past, but incorporates a Real Recovery Expectation, which is a realistic but still hopeful expectation that I've gained during my experience as a recovering anorexic.

As a side note, when I mention the name "Ed," know that it stands for the phrase "eating disorder." This phrase was used by Jenni Schaefer and Thom Rutledge to personify Jenni's eating disorder in their book, *Life Without Ed: How One Woman Declared Independence from Her Eating Disorder and How You Can Too*. From a Christian perspective, Ed is comparable to Satan, whom John described as "the deceiver of the whole world" (Rev. 12:9). Ed's voice can't be audibly heard, but it's definitely loud.

Here's something else that you need to know before you dive into this book: nothing in these pages is a scientific formula. The pages that follow simply include my thoughts and experiences, plus a few passages of Scripture and a few pieces of advice that contribute to the discussion. Please don't think that your recovery will look just like mine because it probably won't.

Everyone with an eating disorder has a unique DNA, a unique experience with Ed, and a unique path to recovery. Thus, you may not need to read every chapter in this book. Or you may not be able to relate to every word that I've written. That's okay and completely normal.

That being said, I believe that no recovery is possible without God. He is our ultimate Healer, and He sustains us as we recover from our eating disorders. He doesn't want us to stay trapped in Satan's lies.

As a final word for this introduction, I want you to know right off the bat that life. Can. Be. Better. I want to tell you that life can become manageable again, even if it doesn't happen overnight. I want you to know that recovery is possible, although it won't be perfect and might not even feel complete. I know from personal experience that recovery from an eating disorder isn't what many people think it is.

I was a pro dieter by the age of sixteen. I could exercise excessively, ignore my hunger signals, and play the comparison game with ease. Calories were my life. And for many years, that was the only life that I knew.

Now that anorexia is (largely) in my rearview mirror, I've realized that there's more to life than calorie charts, clothing sizes, and weight loss goals. On the other hand, I've also realized that recovery is more challenging than I had anticipated.

But "challenging" isn't the same as "not worth it." Trust me when I say that recovery *is* worth it. It's worth the frequent tears, debilitating fears, uncontrollable anger, seeming danger, constant frustration, nervous anticipation, gripping woes, and lowest lows.

If you're going to experience this kind of recovery—*real recovery*—you're going to need real recovery expectations. And that's what this book is all about.

false expectation 1

Once I Start to Recover, I Will Not Mind Gaining Weight

I had had bad days before. Most of them involved standardized testing, allergic reactions, or bear cub encounters. But the *worst* day of my life happened when I was seventeen years old. It was December, which meant that Christmas was coming. Though Christmastime is usually a joyful and exciting time of the year, I was feeling *anything* but joyful and excited.

That was the worst day of my life because I was starting my first legitimate recovery meal plan—the meal plan designed to make me regain the weight that I had worked my butt off to lose. Literally.

By 7:00 p.m. on that cold December day, I had already cried twice—once in the office of my new nutritionist and once in the backseat of my parents' car. (Honestly, I cried a *lot* when I had anorexia and when I was recovering.)

The first time I cried was due to the combination of my new nutritionist giving me a meal plan to recover from my significant weight loss *and* telling me that I had to stop exercising. She was adamant that a cardiologist had to clear me to exercise and that I had to have an electrocardiogram (also known as an EKG) because my heart might be too weak due to my weight loss. Even though I tried to hold back the tears when she said this, I just couldn't.

Exercise meant *everything* to me. Without exercise, I knew that I would gain weight. While my nutritionist was concerned about the health of my heart, I was concerned—actually, terrified—about the size of my stomach.

"You're going to gain so much weight and get so fat!" Ed, my eating disorder, whispered to me.

I continued listening to his voice as my nutritionist began explaining everything that I would have to eat for my new meal plan. The meal plan seemed like it contained an eternally long list of fats, carbohydrates, proteins, dairies, fruits, and vegetables. As she discussed protein options and fat portions, I wasn't listening closely. I was too overwhelmed by my fears.

"Grace, you're going to be a huge fatty when this is over," Ed told me. "You won't even be able to recognize who you are."

I didn't know how I would be able to eat all of the food groups that my nutritionist mentioned—especially if I wanted to maintain my low weight.

I only cried once in the nutritionist's office at the hospital, but I cried again while my parents and I drove home. I couldn't think about anything except how many calories I would be consuming, how many calories I *wouldn't* be burning, and how much my weight would increase as a result. Ed was screaming lies in my head. My emotions were running rampant, and my fears were unappeasable.

When my parents told me to choose something to order at McDonald's a few minutes after we had left the hospital, I couldn't hold back my frustration any longer. I burst into tears because I had to eat a tiny chicken wrap for my new meal plan.

In an hour-long appointment, my life had taken a very drastic turn. In my eyes, it had taken a very drastic turn for the *worse*. And Ed didn't pass up the opportunity to throw punches my way to discourage me.

From my perspective, my new meal plan was earth-shattering. In reality, my new meal plan was rather conservative. It was designed to help me regain weight gradually, not all at once. Yet it felt like I had been told to eat an elephant every day and to never get up from the couch. I was way beyond afraid; I was horrified. Although I couldn't have carried on at my low weight because of the negative consequences for my health that accompanied it, gaining weight was more frightening to me than any health-related consequence from my anorexia.

Needless to say, the first several days—and weeks and months—after I received the new meal plan were very challenging for me. However, it was surprisingly easy to eat all of the required food groups on the meal chart from my nutritionist. I was even hungry *after* I had met all of the requirements, which scared me. Not only was I eating a significantly larger amount of food than I had been eating before, but I was hungry for *additional* food. After writing in what I had eaten on my meal chart, I panicked internally.

How am I not full yet? I thought, frustrated. *I'm definitely gaining weight, but I'm not even eating until I'm satisfied. Maybe my mind is playing tricks on me. Do I have a slow metabolism? Why does my body need this much food?*

At the time, I didn't fully understand my body's hunger and satiated signals. But I *did* understand how I felt. I knew that I loathed my stomach. I knew (or thought that I knew) that it had greatly increased in size since I had stopped exercising. I knew that I wasn't burning off the extra calories that I was consuming. I knew that I hated not exercising but that I had to wait until the cardiologist cleared me to start again.

So, in the meantime, I fussed and fumed. Not surprisingly, I felt more melancholic, more upset, and more depressed—both when I was restricting my eating and when I was using the recovery meal plan.

As I "tried" to regain the weight that I had lost, I still found ways to restrict my eating. At restaurants, my meal often consisted of a grilled chicken salad or a grilled chicken patty. I got severely excited when my family went out to dinner because I allowed myself to eat one of these two bland options. (Woohoo.)

I claimed that I was trying to meet my protein and vegetable requirements for my meal plan. And I was—sort of. Honestly, I was still trying to restrict in the only way that I knew how. I could avoid fried chicken because the calorie content was too high. I could ask for no cheese because it wasn't worth the saturated fat. I could refuse the bread offered on the table because I didn't need any more carbohydrates to meet my meal plan requirements that day.

You might be thinking that my eating habits while I was recovering seem like anorexic eating habits, and you're right. But that was the way that I ate while I followed the meal plan. Skimping a little here. Hiding a little there. Overstating what I had consumed whenever I could get away with it. I cut corners on my recovery meal plan because I didn't want to gain weight. I wasn't attempting to regain the necessary pounds.

Rather, I was still trying to hang onto my restrictive lifestyle.

real recovery expectation

Once I Start to Recover, I Will Let Myself Gain Weight

We'll talk more about this in chapter two, but I want you to recognize something important about the start of my recovery journey. Even though I was mostly following the meal plan that my nutritionist gave me to recover from anorexia, I wasn't completely recovering. My heart, mind, and soul were still very sick, even as I began regaining weight and becoming physically healthy again.

That was true even when I was finally put on weight maintenance. Yes, for about six months, I followed a strict diet and exercise regime to be declared "healthy." Thus, when I arrived at the weight maintenance milestone of my recovery, I expected to feel amazing. But I felt basically the same as I had felt six months ago.

What had changed in those six months of serious physical recovery? Well, I knew how to eat well. I knew how many fats, carbohydrates, proteins, dairies, fruits, and vegetables to consume daily. I knew how to eat balanced meals. My mental state had improved some during this period of recovery.

But even mere weeks before I reached my weight maintenance milestone, I felt deeply discouraged because I hadn't noticed improvement in my anorexic mentality. The thoughts of fatness plagued my mind. I slowly learned that I wasn't fat, but I didn't really believe that I was thin anymore, even though I genuinely was.

Did I have to believe that I was thin to be considered "all better?" Nope. As I will often emphasize in this book, "all better" is an unattainable goal—at least for now. It's a myth that authors, counselors, and doctors like to use to give individuals hope and peace about their recovery. But despite my many years of recovery, I'm still not "all better." And I may never be "all better" if I'm expecting all thoughts of food, exercise, and size to magically disappear from my mind.

As I gained weight throughout my recovery journey, all I wanted was to be skinny. And I wasn't the skinny that I had been previously. My body was perfectly healthy, but in my mind, I might as well have been a sumo wrestler.

I know how indescribably difficult it is to gain weight, even though it's objectively best for your sickly body. But allowing your day, week, month, or year to be ruined because of your weight simply isn't worth the tears. I let small increases in my weight wreck me, and I shouldn't have. It still makes me cringe when I see my weight on the scale, but honestly, no woman gets excited about seeing how much she weighs.

I hated who I had become. You, too, may hate who you become. But never forget who you were. Never forget the body that was always weak from starvation, the body that was in constant pain because it lacked adequate nutrients, the body that was slowly withering away, or the body that didn't hold onto anything except the desire to be still thinner.

What you can expect when you decide to recover from your eating disorder is fear, stress, and frustration. But you can also expect to see progress—even if it's not the kind of progress that you were hoping to see. Be on the lookout for progress of any kind because it's the fuel that'll keep you going during your recovery.

> Not that I have already obtained this or am already perfect, but I press on to make it my own, because Christ Jesus has made me his own. Brothers, I do not consider that I have made it my own. But one thing I do: forgetting what lies behind and straining

forward to what lies ahead, I press on toward the goal for the prize of the upward call of God in Christ Jesus. Let those of us who are mature think this way, and if in anything you think otherwise, God will reveal that also to you. Only let us hold true to what we have attained (Phil. 3:12-16).

Real recovery looks like stepping on the scale and moving on with your day instead of bursting into tears or drowning in depression. It looks like putting your *real* weight on your driver's license instead of pretending to be the weight that you *think* you should be. It looks like weighing yourself only occasionally or not at all instead of weighing yourself daily to make sure that you haven't gained an ounce because I guarantee that your weight will fluctuate slightly and that those slight fluctuations aren't unhealthy or abnormal. It looks like buying clothes that genuinely fit your body well instead of buying baggy clothes that you hope will hide your skin. It looks like accepting the fact that weight gain is necessary to recover instead of panicking that you're going to turn into a sumo wrestler.

After all, individuals with eating disorders rarely end up in that line of work.

false expectation

Food Will Become
My Best Friend

When I had anorexia, I thought about food. All. The. Time.

I couldn't wait until nighttime so that I could plan my meals and my caloric intake for the next day. I read label after label. I became a walking calorie counter. I had memorized the caloric content for countless foods. But if my family went out to a restaurant, I looked up the nutrition facts for its menu items online when my parents and sisters weren't looking. I was disgusted when the nutrition information for the restaurant's menu items wasn't available online.

As an anorexic, I felt like I was lacking. Wanting a little more food, needing a bit more nourishment, craving a little more energy. But I ignored the part of me that wanted a little more food and needed a bit more nourishment and craved a little more energy. I pushed any thoughts of hunger to the back of my mind. After all, hunger is bad, right?

I legitimately wondered if I had a slow metabolism because it took me a while to feel "full." In reality, the feeling of "fullness" that I *did* experience was just my body getting tired of telling me that I was still hungry. My body tried to tell me over and over that I needed more food. When I didn't listen to my body and chose not to eat anymore, it stopped telling me.

To say that my relationship with food was obsessive would be an understatement.

During my years of anorexia, I became fixated on cookbooks and cooking magazines, even though I knew that I shouldn't spend hours looking at them. I bought some of my own, and I read some of my mom's. I just couldn't seem to stop reading them. Honestly, I was infatuated with cookbooks and cooking magazines—especially the ones with lighter options. I borrowed countless cookbooks at a time from our local library. My favorite author wasn't a novelist or a poet; she was a cook who lightened up hundreds of recipes.

In addition to my obsession with cookbooks and cooking magazines, I also spent hours looking at healthy cooking blogs. I bookmarked so many recipes that I couldn't keep track of them. But I didn't actually make the recipes that I had bookmarked.

When I first started restricting what I ate, I did let myself eat family dinners. Whatever my family ate at dinnertime, I also ate. But I was only losing a couple pounds that way, so I began forcing myself to eat "healthy" dinners. I rarely ate my mom's cooking anymore; I would only eat it when it was one of her diet recipes. Otherwise, I just ate something light and pretended that my mom's meals simply weren't my thing.

I also began cooking for myself and my family. The meals I cooked were purposely low-calorie. I used reduced-fat cheese, low-fat sour cream, and other light ingredients to ensure what I ate was low in calories. But baking was different.

I refused to eat the cookies that I baked, even if they were low-fat. When I baked lightened-up sweets for church events or for family members, I declined them. I forced myself to bake them, pack them up, and watch them leave my kitchen without even trying one.

My dad started telling me to eat what I baked, and I said that I would— but I lied. I would either take a teeny bite of one or "save one for later" but throw it away. I constantly lied to my parents and deceived them about what I ate (and about what I didn't eat). Even though I felt guilty, I ignored the Holy Spirit's conviction.

"If you can decline a cookie, you're strong," Ed told me. "And you want to be strong, Grace. Your self-control is what will make you skinny."

At picnics, Ed said that I couldn't eat the brownies, even if everyone else at the picnic was eating them. At church activities, even when I was starving, he told me that I couldn't get a scoop of ice cream or a few chips. At birthday parties, he demanded that I avoid the cake, no matter how awkward I felt about avoiding it. Not surprisingly, I hid from the food table at social events. Family parties, game nights, and church potlucks scared me to death. I didn't know the exact number of calories in the potato salad or the spaghetti or the muffins.

Going to restaurants was always interesting while I had anorexia. When we went out to eat, I often ordered from the kids' menu—which I could get away with because I still looked like a thirteen-year-old—or a salad with grilled chicken. I craved the macaroni and cheese, honey barbecue wings, and mini cheeseburgers. But I viewed those as "bad" foods.

"Those will make you fat," Ed nagged. "They will literally grow fat on your stomach, hips, and butt. Order a cup of chicken noodle soup and a side salad. Make sure you get light dressing on the side, and ask for no bacon bits or cheese on top of the salad."

I ordered water and flavored it with countless slices of lemon. I didn't let myself eat a handful of onion rings or a mini soft pretzel for an appetizer. Ranch dressing, cheese sauce, and honey mustard for dipping were no-nos. Salad was the only "acceptable" item when I ate at a restaurant.

During my eating disorder days, I considered anything that said "nonfat" on the packaging to be a safe option. I also thought that one-hundred-calorie snack packs were wise options, along with one-hundred-calorie English muffins and one-hundred-calorie frozen Greek yogurt bars. I made sure that we had no-sugar-added applesauce and reduced-fat cheese sticks and "healthy white bread" in the kitchen. I figured that even though the foods that I chose to consume probably contained terrible chemicals, at least they didn't contain terrible calories.

Ed made so many demands about my food choices: "Grace, you can't have cheese on your sub." "No sweet tea with your lunch." "No sauce with your chicken nuggets." "No fries with your sandwich." "No milkshake for dessert." "No granola on your yogurt." "Oh, and you can have only light dressing."

Ed added a long list of "onlies" onto that long list of "no-nos": "Only water." "Only salad." "Only one Oreo." "Only skim milk." "Only light salad dressing." "Only diet frozen dinners." "Oh, and you can't eat the meals that your family eats."

I learned to neglect the foods that I used to eat. I never ordered French fries with my meal anymore, and I never had potato chips for a snack. Even though I had gotten mayonnaise on my subs in the past, I learned to live without it and still tolerated the subs. I was semi-content to eat a chicken wrap without ranch, so I asked for it to be left off. Grilled chicken was a lot fewer calories than fried chicken, so I ordered that, too (even though the fried chicken tasted *so* much better).

I didn't hate every single food that I ate. Maybe I couldn't get the fried chicken and cheese sandwich at Bob Evans, but I could get a kids' cheeseburger. I couldn't get the macaroni and cheese at Panera Bread, but I could get half of a grilled cheese sandwich. I couldn't order the chicken nuggets at Wendy's, but I could order the small barbecue chicken salad. They were still tasty-*ish* choices.

Day after day, all that I did was deny myself the foods that I craved and pretend that I was satisfied with other options. I learned to make sacrifices as an anorexic. And I learned to be a master resister. My self-control definitely grew through my anorexia—but not in a good way. When my body said, "Feed me!," I replied, "You can wait," which meant no.

Ignoring my hunger was one of the main reasons that I lost weight, but it was also one of the main reasons that my body became weak.

real recovery expectation

Food Will No Longer Be My Worst Enemy

Once I started using the recovery meal plan from my nutritionist, I started eating differently but still not well. I filled in the food group boxes on that meal chart, but I was too scared to eat a single calorie more than necessary. I couldn't take any chances. After all, evil calories lead to weight gain, right?

During that point in my recovery, I ate the leanest proteins—chicken, turkey, and egg whites—even though they were really bland. I never ate cheese, eggs, bacon, or ground beef. They were too high in fat, according to Ed at least. And since non-lean meats couldn't count as a protein *and* a fat on my meal chart, I avoided them like the plague.

I remember bawling over a Subway salad during my recovery because I *really* didn't want to eat it. I wasn't afraid of the spinach or the lettuce. I was afraid of the cheese on top. In my eyes, it was a mountain of cheese, full of calories and saturated fat. In reality, it was a simple but flavorful salad topping with protein and calcium.

As you can tell, my obsession with food didn't suddenly disappear when I started eating more food and giving my body the nutrition that it needed. I still knew every trick in the diet book. I knew about drinking a glass of water before meals to feel less hungry, eating an apple to instantly satisfy my hunger, and chewing gum to calm down my growling stomach, especially before a meal.

Sure, I knew that other people could simply eat without obsessing about it. But I pondered, analyzed, and dissected what I ate.

If I ate anything that Ed told me was "bad," I felt guilty. I thought about the weight that I might gain and the calories that I would have to burn to make up for my "unhealthy" choices. I was convinced that certain foods would make me fatter. I believed Ed when he told me to avoid them at all costs.

I didn't eat cheese for months, even though I loved it. Chocolate was off-limits, even though it was delicious. I severely limited my ice cream intake, even though it was my favorite dessert. I fell for Ed's schemes that greens are the only acceptable food on this earth.

I can't describe the guilt that I felt after I made brownies and ate two of them. You would've thought that I had consumed half the pan by the amount of wallowing that I did over just three hundred calories' worth of brownies. I inwardly lamented because I knew that it would take me forever to exercise away the delicious brownies.

I'm sure that you've experienced that kind of guilt before—that degrading, gut-wrenching, yet unnecessary guilt. Honestly, I hate that our society doesn't allow us to eat a brownie or a milkshake or a cheeseburger. What's so wrong with ordering French fries *instead* of a side salad? What's the matter with choosing a chocolate chip cookie *instead* of an orange? Why is nonfat, no-sugar-added *always* the best choice? And what *does* society allow us to eat without condemnation? Kale, wheat bran, fish, and coconut oil. Ooh, goody. Lean proteins, whole grains, and vegetables get really boring really quickly.

But society isn't the only cause of our food worries. So is Ed.

"Cheese is evil, Grace," Ed lied to me. "Chocolate is evil. Ice cream is evil. Pizza is evil. Beef is evil. They're not safe foods, Grace. Those foods will widen your hips, enlarge your thighs, and swell your stomach. Those foods are wretched, and you need to avoid them at all costs."

I should've told Ed that *he* is the wretched one to avoid at all costs. And interestingly, what he failed to tell me was that those foods *don't* cause weight gain when they're consumed *in moderation*. He also failed to tell me that strictly avoiding those foods would keep me in bondage to calories—and to him.

> What then? Are we to sin because we are not under law but under grace? By no means! Do you not know that if you present yourselves to anyone as obedient slaves, you are slaves of the one whom you obey, either of sin, which leads to death, or of obedience, which leads to righteousness? But thanks be to God, that you who were once slaves of sin have become obedient from the heart to the standard of teaching to which you were committed, and, having been set free from sin, have become slaves of righteousness. I am speaking in human terms, because of your natural limitations. For just as you once presented your members as slaves to impurity and to lawlessness leading to more lawlessness, so now present your members as slaves to righteousness leading to sanctification. For when you were slaves of sin, you were free in regard to righteousness. But what fruit were you getting at that time from the things of which you are now ashamed? For the end of those things is death. But now that you have been set free from sin and have become slaves of God, the fruit you get leads to sanctification and its end, eternal life. For the wages of sin is death, but the free gift of God is eternal life in Christ Jesus our Lord (Rom. 6:15-23).

Real recovery looks like slowly but steadily incorporating "scary" foods into your diet instead of banishing them to the back of the pantry. It looks like forcing yourself to eat a full serving of whatever you cook or bake instead of taking a nibble of it and throwing out the rest. It looks like avoiding analysis of online and print nutrition labels instead of studying them like a calculus textbook. It looks like canceling your subscriptions to all cooking magazines and food blogs instead of letting yourself browse them for hours but never making what looks appealing. It looks like deleting all of your calorie-counting apps instead of tracking every tiny peanut that you consume.

After all, a three-calorie peanut doesn't really translate into three added pounds of weight or three added inches to your waistline.

false expectation
I Will Exercise to Have Fun

Honestly, I don't even remember when I started working out my abs. But I do remember that I was adamant about doing it.

I looked at websites with pictures and videos of men and women doing planks, V-ups, and sit-ups. I wanted their rock-hard abs and flat stomachs. I wanted to look that amazing in a sports bra and tiny shorts. I read articles and watched videos with titles like, "Ten Great Exercises for a Flat Stomach" and "The Best Five-Minute Workout for Sexy Abs" and "Twenty Ways to Lose Your Belly Fat." The titles reeled me in. I was desperate to attain a body that, in reality, didn't exist.

Although I despised my ab workouts almost as much as I despised my stomach, I forced myself to regularly have a targeted workout. I did exercises like crunches, V-ups, and planks with the hope that I would get a flat stomach. And as my recovery progressed, I actually increased the amount of time that I did my targeted workouts because I became so fearful that my stomach would get bigger and because I started hating even more body parts.

I stuck with one routine for a while that seemed to flatten my stomach, but when I thought that I stopped seeing results, I quit that routine and tried a new one. I felt like some workouts were even making me fatter. What I failed to acknowledge at the time was that working out builds muscle, hence my increased "fatness." I also failed to acknowledge that a flat stomach is only possible on a skeletally thin body.

"Why isn't your stomach flat yet?" Ed asked me constantly. "What are you doing wrong? You need a new workout. A *longer* workout. A *harder* workout. A *better* workout."

To be honest, I spent *way* too much time looking at workouts. I just wanted to find the perfect workout that would give me a toned tummy.

Would I get a toned tummy if I did sit-ups or crunches? Would working out my abs four days a week for an hour or seven days a week for half an hour provide the outcome that I wanted? Would a missed workout result in a flabby stomach, or would a missed workout have minimal consequences?

During my journey through anorexia and the recovery that followed, I also started doing hip workouts and arm workouts (in addition to the ab workouts that I had started doing before my recovery) because I hated my hips and arms. If I had had my way, I would've started spot training every area of my body because I essentially hated everything about it, except my dimples and my wrists (because dimples are just adorable and because I could see my wrist bone through each of my wrists). But just like with the ab workouts that I did so religiously, no matter how many times I did pretzel crunches or lifted weights, I still hated my hips and arms passionately—even as I recovered.

For aerobic exercise, I biked consistently on my mom's stationary bike for at least half an hour every single day—even on Thanksgiving. To feel like I had biked enough, I had to burn a very specific number of calories that Ed arbitrarily demanded from me. I felt super guilty if I didn't exercise, so biking became my first priority. It was all that mattered to me (besides my ab workouts, of course).

When I went off to college and was at a healthier weight, I decided to try running. After all, everyone seemed to be a runner. And running burned a *ton* of calories, so I gave it a shot—and I failed miserably.

My knees couldn't handle it. I got runner's knee and had to live on ibuprofen for two weeks. I kept an ice pack and a heating pad nearby for when I couldn't handle the pain. For weeks, my knees throbbed as I walked to my classes, the cafeteria, and the library.

But I was stubborn. I desperately wanted to be a runner. I wanted people to see me running and think, "Wow, she has such a great runner's body. She's so athletic." I wanted to burn five hundred calories in thirty minutes from running instead of burning 250 calories from walking or jogging the same amount of time.

So, after my knees healed, I tried running again. And the same thing happened: I hurt my body. The pain in my knees was terrible, and all that I could do to ease the pain was find an icepack and take ibuprofen. As much as I hated to admit it, I didn't have the body for running. My knees were simply too weak.

"Wow, Grace," Ed scolded me. "All of your friends are runners. You're the only one who's not. They can burn five hundred calories without giving it a second thought. You can only walk on the treadmill like a fifty-year-old woman."

Ed tormented me about the ways that I exercised and about the amount of time that I exercised. He told me what sports were better than others. So, for example, when a friend started offering tennis lessons to my family, I started going to the tennis courts twice a week. But I was annoyed that I didn't burn as many calories on the tennis court as I did on the stationary bike.

Even though I had heard that being in the sunshine could improve my mental health and that exercising in a group is a good idea, all that I cared about was burning a lot of calories.

real recovery expectation

I Will Exercise to Burn a Moderate Number of Calories

I hated when I read that I should exercise "for the fun of it." Or that I should enjoy the way that exercise makes my body feel. Or that I should exercise for the goal of health and wellness. I thought that those expectations were silly and basically impossible to have.

And I honestly *still* think that those expectations are kind of silly and basically impossible to have. Does that mean that I shouldn't exercise? Nope. Does that mean that I should exercise excessively? Definitely nope. Most forms of exercise aren't particularly enjoyable. After all, working out causes me to sweat excessively. It leaves me exhausted. It sometimes makes my body hurt.

When I had anorexia, I worked out to burn the calories that I consumed. Today, post-anorexia, I still work out to burn the calories that I consume. And that's okay.

It's okay if you're in the same boat as I am. You can work out to burn calories. Perhaps that's one reason why you never see people smiling at the gym—because they're working out to burn calories, not to have fun. But you should never work out *excessively* to burn *all* of the calories that you have consumed or will consume in a day.

What's the magic number that determines how much exercise is best for your body? Only your doctor and your God-given instincts can tell you. If your body tells you, "Hey, you're pushing me too hard," then listen. If your body says, "Hey, I hurt way too much," then listen. If your body warns you, "Hey, that last workout almost killed me," then listen.

Likewise, if you truly trust your doctor (who has been in school for decades, by the way), then you'll listen when he says that you should cut back on your exercise. You'll listen when she says that your feet always hurt because you run too much. You'll listen when she says that you're burning too many calories during your workouts.

Also, just to let you know, there's absolutely nothing holy about running. Despite its current popularity in society (which may only last for another year or month or week), the possible negative side effects of running are painful and serious in the long-term.

Running isn't a sin (unless it becomes an idol), but don't force your body to do something that it's not meant to do or to become something that it's not meant to become. I've tried that, and it's miserable. If you can run without pain, then run. If you can walk without pain, then walk. Hike, swim, jog, dance, or use the elliptical. Play soccer, basketball, volleyball, tennis, softball, hockey, or lacrosse.

A little temporary pain might be fine. But even though I'm not an athletic trainer, I know that consistent or severe pain *isn't* fine. Stop whatever exercise is causing it. Hurting your body long-term isn't worth the fact that you can call yourself a runner. In a few years, that runner status won't matter. Your physical health still will. And so will your spiritual health.

> For while bodily training is of some value, godliness is of value in every way, as it holds promise for the present life and also for the life to come. The saying is trustworthy and deserving of full acceptance. For to this end we toil and strive, because we have our hope set on the living God, who is the Savior of all people, especially of those who believe (1 Tim. 4:8-10).

Real recovery looks like letting yourself skip a day of exercise every now and then instead of forcing yourself to exercise every single day. It looks like wearing athletic gear without a trendy logo instead of wearing only Nike and Adidas clothing so that everyone will think that you're athletic. It looks like choosing a variety of ways to exercise, like walking or playing tennis or kayaking, instead of restricting your exercise to running because it burns a lot of calories. It looks like setting aside time to spend with Jesus in the morning instead of brushing aside your quiet time to go for a run. It looks like selling your Fitbit instead of checking it every five minutes to see how many calories you've burned.

> After all, you'll probably burn more
> calories pumping your arms while you
> exercise than checking your Fitbit.

false expectation

I Will Feel Good in my New, Healthy Body

When my eating disorder specialist at Children's National Hospital told me that I had anorexia nervosa, I was actually pretty happy to hear it. I felt like I had *achieved* an eating disorder—like I had attained the status of a winner. I had lost enough weight to be considered anorexic.

"Go you," Ed applauded me. "You really accomplished something here, Grace. You should be proud of yourself."

But his praise was quite sporadic.

When I visited the cardiologist during the early months of my recovery, I felt like I hadn't accomplished *anything*. I was sitting in his office because my nutritionist had told me that I couldn't exercise until the cardiologist had cleared me to exercise. My nutritionist was worried that my heart was too weak for me to handle even nonaerobic exercise, so I had to see a cardiologist for a stress test and an EKG.

When I went to see the cardiologist, he asked me and my parents to explain what had happened with the anorexia. My parents shared how much weight I had lost, but my heart dropped when the cardiologist said that I probably hadn't lost enough weight to severely damage my heart. I know that's a terrible thing for me to have been disappointed about, but I was.

And Ed didn't hold back from sharing his helpful commentary with me.

"Wow, Grace," Ed hissed. "You really failed here, didn't you? You didn't do anything dramatic. You didn't get the best body. You just went on a little diet. You were essentially an unsuccessful anorexic. Way to go."

I should've told Ed that my physical symptoms revealed that I had actually been a very "successful" anorexic. Even better, I should've told Ed that developing an eating disorder is a slow suicide, not an accomplishment.

The clearest indication that my anorexic habits were harming my physical health was that I didn't have my menstrual period—for way too long. Honestly, I don't remember how long I didn't have my period. I just remember that it didn't come, and it continued to *not* come. It didn't come back until I had physically recovered from anorexia.

My paleness was another indication of my failing physical health. I had always had fair skin, which my family compared to the complexion of a china doll when I was healthy. But when I was anorexic, my family thought that I looked eerily pale. They were worried about my suddenly white skin tone.

Likewise, my sunken eyes revealed my unhealthy, low weight. My face was getting thinner, which made my eyes look sunken. I didn't really notice, but my family definitely did.

My flaky nails also indicated that my physical health was deteriorating. Because having smooth nails isn't an absolutely essential bodily function, my body moved onto more pressing issues. Thus, my nails peeled instead of growing smoothly and healthily.

Another indication of my worsening physical health was that my hair was flat and wouldn't grow. I had always had short, thin hair. My hair grew really slowly, and I just had to accept that fact as a child. But during my teen years when my body was supposed to be growing and thriving, my hair refused to get longer. Hair growth isn't an essential bodily function, after all.

Clearly, my body wasn't happy that I was pursuing the "perfect" body. My body wasn't well enough to have a menstrual period, vibrant skin, bright eyes, shiny nails, or growing hair. My body had to spend every calorie that I consumed on its essential functions, like pumping blood to my heart and helping me breathe. (By the way, I put the word "perfect" in quotation marks because Ed wants us to believe that the ideal body exists and that we can attain the ideal body if we follow his rules. News flash—the ideal body doesn't exist, and we can never attain the ideal body because the "ideal body" concept is so subjective.)

Perhaps there were other negative physical side effects from having an eating disorder that I didn't even notice. But the physical side effects that I *did* notice led to me spending a lot of time in hospitals and doctors' offices. To be specific, I had frequent appointments with my general practitioner and my nutritionist. I had multiple visits to Children's National Hospital to see an eating disorder specialist. I had to have a stress test, an EKG, a bone density scan, and lab work done.

But I didn't just see them while I was anorexic. I also saw them while I was physically recovering from anorexia *and* while I was physically recovered from anorexia. My appointments with them played an important role in my physical recovery, but I honestly didn't like how my body was changing from anorexic to healthy.

My body disgusted me in the depths of anorexia *and* in the depths of recovery. To this day, my body disgusts me. And if there was a stronger word for disgust, I would use it.

Both in my anorexic mind and in my post-anorexic mind, my stomach seemed to bulge—especially compared to everyone else's stomachs. If I ventured outside of my mind, I knew that my stomach wasn't fat in the least. That fact didn't matter to me, though. I still hated my stomach.

The hatred I had for my body during anorexia was the same hatred I had for my body during recovery. I was completely dissatisfied with my reflection in the mirror. I checked myself out from the front, the sides, and the back. But every angle disgusted me. I just wanted to look like a stick because that's what looked good to me, and it seemed like everyone looked like a stick except for me.

To cope with the body hatred that I had as I struggled with anorexia and with recovery, I physically hurt my body. Therefore, not surprisingly, I went to bed in pain and woke up in pain. Sometimes, I randomly felt a sharp pain shoot up my side. Certain body parts ached or throbbed. And *I* was the cause of my pain.

The methods that I used to try to control how my body looked and felt were my own form of cutting. I was too scared to cut myself, so I did everything else to subject and torture it. Even today, with anorexia years behind me, I still struggle with hurting my body.

Likewise, I struggle with seeing my body in an objective way. I couldn't see myself objectively, even when my doctors told me what they saw objectively. Shockingly, Ed never spoke to me that way. During my appointments when my doctors expressed concerns that I hadn't gained enough weight or that I shouldn't be focusing so much on counting calories, Ed took advantage of those opportunities to lie to me.

"All I see is fat when I look at you," Ed said to me. "Your stomach is gross. Your hips are wide. Your arms are ugly. Your legs are flabby. Your doctors don't know what they're talking about."

The further that I progressed in my recovery, the more positive the feedback from my doctors became. My general practitioner, nutritionist, and eating disorder specialist didn't worry as much about me anymore. Although they had expressed concerns about my low weight in the past, they didn't seem as concerned as they used to be. Their voices were less fearful and more pleased.

But honestly, I was far from pleased with how my body was recovering. It didn't feel healthy; it felt fat. I felt gross and uncomfortable in my own skin. I obsessed about how my body felt, and I still do sometimes.

It's difficult to explain the sensations that I experienced, but perhaps you can understand what I mean. It seemed like I could feel myself with every movement that I made. I was uber conscious of certain body parts, like my stomach and my thighs. No item of clothing felt comfortable or flattering on me. Whether I wore a loose t-shirt or a pair of tight skinny jeans, I felt utterly hideous. I wasn't supposed to feel hideous when I returned to a healthy weight.

I was supposed to feel *good*. But I didn't.

real recovery expectation
I Will Feel Safe in My New, Healthy Body

Thankfully, I never had to be admitted to a hospital or stay at a recovery facility because of my anorexia. It wasn't as severe as it could've been. God kept me from hurting myself more than I did. In fact, He preserved my life.

According to my general practitioner, I lost the equivalent of twenty pounds because of my weight loss combined with my height increase. As I regained those pounds (plus a few more) during my recovery, I struggled greatly. I wanted to be skinny more than anything else, and the negative side effects that resulted from being too skinny made me feel oddly proud. Every pound that I regained became an opportunity for Ed to scold me.

"Why are you giving this up?" Ed whispered in my ear. "I know that your body isn't thriving right now, but you're just trying to achieve something beautiful, okay? Don't give up now, Grace."

From Ed's point of view, I was giving up on my goal of being thin. Of being the slender girl in the room. Of having a skinnier body than her and her and her. But something happened inside my body when I decided that I didn't have to be those things—my body became happy again.

I got my menstrual period after not having it for years. The color returned to my skin. Life returned to my eyes. My nails didn't peel as much anymore. And perhaps most significantly to me, my hair miraculously started to grow.

That might not sound very miraculous to you, but let me explain. Ever since I had been a little girl, my hair had been short and thin. I had never cut it more than a few inches because it took an eternity to grow back. I basically kept it at shoulder-length because it never grew beyond that. I was envious of my friends' fast-growing hair because they were able to donate it frequently to organizations that made wigs for cancer patients. I envied my older sister's hair and my younger sister's hair because they seemed to grow so long while mine seemed like it would be short forever. It was always my desire to have long, luscious, blonde hair.

It wasn't particularly odd that my hair stayed short and thin while I was depriving my body of the nutrients that it needed to thrive. But when I made the choice to recover from my eating disorder, the miracle happened. *My hair grew over twelve inches.*

I didn't get the long, luscious, blonde hair that I had always wanted *until* I started to recover from my eating disorder. When I chose recovery, my blonde hair became long and luscious. Just like I had always wanted. The change was truly incredible.

As a child, I would've been pleased if my hair had grown *three* inches. I never would've imagined that it would grow *twelve* inches. Having long hair was a dream come true for me, and it wouldn't have been possible if I had continued following Ed's demands.

Since my hair's "growth spurt," countless people have mentioned how long my hair has gotten. One of my friends *still* comments about how long it is when I see her. Perhaps God is using her to remind me of the work that He has done through my recovery.

It's remarkable what can happen when you choose to recover from your eating disorder.

Of course, you probably won't appreciate every part of your physical recovery. For example, even though I prayed for my period to come back consistently, I secretly hoped that it wouldn't. I actually became frightened when it did return on a regular basis. I secretly wanted to be different. To be special. To be the girl with the irregular period. I liked the attention that I got when my period didn't come—even though it wasn't really *good* attention.

I felt like a "successful" anorexic if my period didn't come for a month or two. I felt like perhaps I was actually skinny if I didn't have it every month. Internally, I beat myself up about having a period for several months in a row. Not only that, but a regular period meant having painful cramps, buying tons of maxi pads, getting depressed, and feeling fatter than I usually felt.

But everyone else was thrilled when my period returned. My parents, sisters, and doctors celebrated. They were so pleased that my body was proclaiming, "I'm healthy again!" Meanwhile, I felt like proclaiming, "But I want to be skinny again!"

However, God reminded me (via my family, friends, and doctors) that having a regular period meant that I could start a family someday, that having rosy skin meant that I didn't look sickly anymore, that having bright eyes meant that I could smile and look sincere, that having smooth nails meant that I wasn't distracted by their constant flakiness, and that having long, blonde hair meant that God had given me the desire of my heart.

> Fret not yourself because of evildoers; be not envious of wrongdoers! For they will soon fade like the grass and wither like the green herb. Trust in the LORD, and do good; dwell in the land and befriend faithfulness. Delight yourself in the LORD, and he will give you the desires of your heart. Commit your way to the LORD; trust in him, and he will act. He will bring forth your righteousness as the light, and your justice as the noonday (Psalm 37:1-6).

Real recovery looks like taking a step back from the mirror long enough to recognize your well-being or lack of well-being instead of naïvely believing that how you see yourself in the mirror determines it. It looks like going to your doctors faithfully—no matter how difficult it is to listen to them—instead of putting up a fight every time your mom schedules an appointment for you. It looks like accepting the physical realities of womanhood, like painful periods and wrinkly cellulite, instead of agonizing over them. It looks like trusting what your doctors and loved ones tell you about your physical health instead of trusting what Ed tells you about your physical health. It looks like making sure that you feel *safe* in your own skin instead of making sure that you feel *comfortable* in your own skin.

After all, if you aren't safe in your own skin, you may be mistaken for a ghost, a witch, or a skeleton on Halloween—none of which are great costumes.

false expectation

I Will No Longer Hear Lies From Ed

Before I developed an eating disorder, the hardest parts of my life were trying to understand geometry, stubbing my toes on various pieces of furniture, and making curls stay in my hair for longer than fifteen minutes. Until Ed started whispering to me and I started listening to him.

As I explained in the introduction, Satan speaks to you using the voice of Ed—your eating disorder. And the torment from Ed was constant in my life. He didn't just torment me while I was in the depths of anorexia; he also tormented me while I was in the depths of recovery. Ed's lies continually filled my mind.

God did bless me with moments of peace. There were even a couple days when I didn't feel hatred for my body. But those days were few and far between.

I don't understand why the torment never goes away, I thought angrily. *Why do I always feel bad about myself? Will I ever feel "normal" again? Will I ever feel satisfied with the body that God designed for me?*

I highly doubted it.

Like I said, there were a few amazing days when I didn't hate how I looked. When I didn't scold myself for eating two thousand calories instead of the fifteen hundred calories that Ed wanted me to eat. When I didn't lecture myself for only exercising fifteen minutes instead of the sixty minutes that Ed wanted me to exercise.

For those few amazing days of relief, I felt okay with myself. I didn't feel like a fatso. But I was cautiously optimistic during those days because I knew that my negative emotions and Ed's torment could increase exponentially at any moment.

And sure enough, they did. I went back to hating myself. I returned to the scolding and the lecturing. Actually, I returned to Ed so that *he* could scold and lecture me. The world seemed like a very dark place when every doctor, nutritionist, counselor, and family member in my life was telling me to *gain* weight because I was too thin, while Ed was telling me to *lose* weight because I was too fat.

Nothing made sense to me during those first few months of my recovery. They were so difficult. All I could do was fill in the food group boxes on the meal chart that my nutritionist had designed for me and hear the chiding from Ed before, during, and after.

My life was a blur of hunger and body hatred. I was finally giving my body the nutrients that it needed to thrive, but I couldn't stand myself for doing it. My food intake, my workout routine, and my weight were becoming normal. But my mind was a wreck. All I could hear was lie after lie.

As my recovery continued and I transitioned from filling in food group boxes on a meal chart to tracking calories throughout the day, I hoped that Ed's voice would become quieter. After all, I was physically healthy again. I figured that I would also become emotionally, mentally, and spiritually healthy again.

But I didn't. Ed didn't want to loosen his grip on me. In fact, it felt like his grip on me was getting tighter. The physical progress that I was making probably stimulated Ed to increase his efforts to cause me harm.

His grip felt especially tight during a family trip to the beach. Honestly, vacations are always scary for me because they're relatively unstructured and quite fluid. During vacation, it's hard to consistently eat healthy and squeeze in time for daily workouts. Desserts are available everywhere, and relaxation is prioritized over physical exertion.

But on that particular vacation, I didn't expect to feel so much false guilt. Even though I had been maintaining a healthy weight for a few years at that point and I wasn't quite as obsessed about my body as I used to be, the trip was incredibly difficult for me. I was frustrated with myself for no logical reason.

Why am I not okay? I asked myself. *I started my recovery long ago. Shouldn't I be okay with all of this?*

But I wasn't. Eating on vacation was super hard that time. Ed gave me flack about every calorie that I put in my mouth and every calorie that I didn't burn. My mind was racing throughout the day instead of resting. I definitely focused way too much on my meals, exercise, and body during the vacation.

Although that was an especially hard trip for me, I didn't just struggle then. I struggled *daily*. The lies hurt my body, mind, heart, and soul.

When my counselor finally told me that I should consider taking an anti-depressant or anxiety medication, I was pleased. My general practitioner prescribed a very low dosage of an anxiety drug to assist me with my obsessive-compulsive disorder and the anxiety that I had about my body. I thought that I would finally stop hearing Ed's voice that was constantly ringing in my ear. I believed that a pill would somehow "cure" me of his lies. But that's not what the pill did.

Instead, I felt about the same as I had felt before I started taking the anxiety medication. My mind was still filled with Ed's lies. My heart was still filled with negativity. My soul was still filled with false guilt. Even taking a larger dose of the anxiety medication didn't silence Ed.

Thus, I came to the conclusion that nothing would.

real recovery expectation
I Will No Longer Let Ed Control Every Decision I Make

One of my counselors taught me the importance of paying attention to my thoughts and determining the truth when my thoughts don't align with the truth. So, during my recovery, I wrote down what I was hearing in my head and what I should be believing instead. Maybe you've heard some of the same lies that I heard, and maybe you need to hear some of the same truths that I did.

> Lie from Ed: "You know that skin on your hips and ribs? That's actually fat."

> Truth to combat Ed's lie: "I need skin to protect my bones and joints. I can't be a body of bones. A healthy person needs skin. I'm a beautiful, healthy person, and I need skin. I'm on the *thin* end of healthy."

> Lie from Ed: "If you don't exercise today, you'll gain weight and get fat."

> Truth to combat Ed's lie: "If I make a habit of not exercising, I'll probably gain weight."

> Lie from Ed: "You're so fat. Has anyone told you how ugly you are?"

> Truth to combat Ed's lie: "Only *you* have told me that I'm ugly, and you're a liar."

The truths I had to tell myself were mostly things that my counselors had taught me. Honestly, I wasn't very encouraged by the truths I wrote down to combat the lies I heard. But I wrote them down, anyway. You, too, may struggle to believe the truths that you write down to combat the lies that you hear. But write them down, anyway. Because Ed's lies aren't just words; they're weapons.

Here's the thing—when Ed lies to you, his aim isn't to give you a better body. Rather, his aim is to *destroy* your body. If you're a follower of Christ, Ed can't have your soul (John 10:27-29). However, Ed *can* lead you to destroy your body (John 10:10).

That's something that my parents told me a while ago. My mom said that Ed wanted me to hurt myself because he couldn't physically hurt me. My dad said that anorexia is a slow suicide because it steals your life one day at a time and is miserable for you and everyone around you. It makes perfect sense if you think about it. Ed wants to use *you* to destroy your *own* body. And with every restricted calorie and every excessive workout, you let him.

I could fill your head with statistics about how many people die from eating disorders or how many people end up in the hospital because of eating disorders. (It's a lot, by the way.) But I'm not here to fill your head with statistics. After all, the last thing that you're probably going to pay attention to is more statistics—especially if Ed is whispering lies in your ear.

Ed promises that you won't be one of the statistics. He convinces you that he won't let your eating disorder kill you. He assures you that you won't end up in a hospital room or in a coffin like the others.

I wish that I could promise you the same things that Ed promises you, but I can't.

Anyone can develop an eating disorder, and anyone can die from an eating disorder. There was absolutely no reason why I should develop an eating disorder. The only plausible reason why I did was feeling out-of-control about the future and thus feeling the need to control something in my life.

But I grew up in a home where I was frequently told how much I was loved and how beautiful I was. I saw a pediatrician who always said that I was perfectly healthy. There was no abuse, bullying, or criticism in my life. Just love, praise, and affection. I didn't show any warning signs.

So why did Ed come to me? Why did I choose to listen to him? There was no clear cause-and-effect process. It all happened so fast—and yet so gradually. My parents didn't even notice that I had developed an eating disorder until I was years into the process. I was incredibly secretive about how much I was eating and exercising.

Ed appreciates the art of secret-keeping. He likes to hide in the shadows where he can influence you without being discovered. The darkness is his home, and he wants you to stay with him. I stayed with him for a while (which you can read more about in chapter eight).

I thought that he would give me what I wanted—a skinny body. Eventually, he did. But I had to work hard for that skinny body. And my hard work somehow didn't seem to pay off because my skinny body didn't seem *quite* skinny enough. Thankfully, I listened to God's call and walked out of the darkness. (Okay, I didn't walk; I crawled.) But Ed wasn't happy about it.

"Remember the good old days of your anorexia, Grace?" Ed hissed. "Remember when your ribs were *way* more visible than they are now? Remember when you could fit into that tiny shirt from the juniors' department? Remember when you owned those tiny shorts from the girls' department? Didn't that feel good?"

Still, all that Ed had to offer me were arbitrary rules, dangerous lies, and cruel bondage. There was no freedom with him. But there was with God.

The first day that I filled in the food group boxes on my meal chart was the first day that I heard Ed's voice *and* ignored it. Without realizing it at the time, Jesus' words to the Jews thousands of years ago were becoming a reality in my life. The truth set me free.

So Jesus said to the Jews who had believed him, "If you abide in my word, you are truly my disciples, and you will know the truth, and the truth will set you free." They answered him, "We are offspring of Abraham and have never been enslaved to anyone. How is it that you say, 'You will become free'?" Jesus answered them, "Truly, truly, I say to you, everyone who practices sin is a slave to sin. The slave does not remain in the house forever; the son remains forever. So if the Son sets you free, you will be free indeed. I know that you are offspring of Abraham; yet you seek to kill me because my word finds no place in you. I speak of what I have seen with my Father, and you do what you have heard from your father." They answered him, "Abraham is our father." Jesus said to them, "If you were Abraham's children, you would be doing the works Abraham did, but now you seek to kill me, a man who has told you the truth that I heard from God. This is not what Abraham did. You are doing the works your father did." They said to him, "We were not born of sexual immorality. We have one Father—even God." Jesus said to them, "If God were your Father, you would love me, for I came from God and I am here. I came not of my own accord, but he sent me. Why do you not understand what I say? It is because you cannot bear to hear my word. You are of your father the devil, and your will is to do your father's desires. He was a murderer from the beginning, and does not stand in the truth, because there is no truth in him. When he lies, he speaks out of his own character, for he is a liar and the father of lies. But because I tell the truth, you do not believe me. Which one of you convicts me of sin? If I tell the truth, why do you not believe me? Whoever is of God hears the words of God. The reason why you do not hear them is that you are not of God" (John 8:31-47).

Real recovery looks like finding out what the truth is from the God Who loves you unconditionally, the family members and friends who care about you deeply, and the doctors and counselors who are trained to assist you skillfully, instead of assuming that Ed knows the truth. It looks like making a list of reasons why Ed isn't trustworthy, starting with Scripture as a resource, instead of rationalizing why Ed is trustworthy. It looks like choosing to ignore the voice of Ed—no matter how loud his voice is—instead of choosing to follow the voice of Ed. It looks like doing the exact opposite of what Ed demands you to do—whether it's going on a walk instead of a run, deleting all of your social media accounts instead of browsing them for hours, or eating a cheeseburger instead of a salad for lunch—instead of doing the exact thing that Ed demands you to do. It looks like gathering Bible verses, words from your family members and friends, and guidance from your doctors and counselors to use as weapons in your fight against Ed's lies instead of consuming his lies like candy.

After all, if you consume his lies like candy, you'll rot your soul—and maybe your teeth, too.

false expectation

I Will Love How My New, Healthy Body Looks

In a world of pretzel sticks, I saw myself as a marshmallow. During my journey through anorexia and my journey through recovery, I couldn't see myself objectively—especially in comparison to other people. In actuality, I was one of the thin girls. But that's not how I saw myself.

I knew how rude it was to categorize people based on their looks. I knew how offensive it was to paint people with a broad brush based on how I felt in the moment. I knew how un-Christian it was to describe people the way that I described them. Still, although my thoughts about others were incredibly rude, offensive, and un-Christian, my thoughts about myself were even worse.

As an anorexic *and* as a recovering anorexic, I believed that I was losing the comparison game. Everyone seemed skinnier than I was. The girls I saw at the mall, in restaurants, and at the movie theater all looked thin, and—from my skewed perspective—I looked fat. Something I didn't understand was how my skinny friends seemed to be able to eat whatever they wanted.

During a youth group trip, I was especially frustrated that everyone was eating junk food while I was eating healthy food. Yet they *still* looked thin, and I *still* felt fat.

Ugh, I thought, irritated. *How come everyone can eat all of this junk food and still be skinny? I have to eat a bland yogurt parfait while the skinny people chow down on cheeseburgers and fries. I want fries.*

On the other hand, when I attended a homeschool tutorial in high school, I noticed that several of the girls there looked like sticks and that they never really ate anything. It seemed like if I tapped them, they would fall over because they were so thin. Honestly, they were unhealthily thin. Those girls were nice, but I didn't like hanging out with them because it reminded me of how "fat" I was. And by "fat," I mean "objectively thin." I didn't have a logical understanding of my size, especially in comparison to their sizes.

Whether my friends were eating French fries and drinking milkshakes or nibbling on carrot sticks and throwing out their pizza slices, I never felt like I would win the comparison game.

When I took an introductory college psychology class, I began to understand why. In my textbook for the class, I noticed a really intriguing illustration that perfectly captured my struggle. The illustration depicted a young woman who was rail-thin. However, when she looked in the mirror, she saw a young woman who was obese.

I felt *exactly* like the girl in that illustration, but I honestly think that everyone with an eating disorder feels like that woman.

The mirror was certainly my rival, but my reflection was my mortal enemy. *I* disgusted me. When I looked in the mirror, I saw a centaur—a half-man, half-horse creature. Plump. Hideous. Needing to stay hidden, like Mr. Tumnus in *The Lion, the Witch, and the Wardrobe.* From my perspective, I was a fatso with a potbelly and wide hips. From the perspective of everyone else, I was a pretty girl who could wear anything that she wanted and look great. But I couldn't see what they saw.

When will I finally be satisfied with who I am? I agonized.

It was definitely difficult to be satisfied with who *I* was when I was so focused on who *other people* were.

When I was in college (and technically "recovered" from anorexia), chapel was actually a really hard place for me to be. At my small Christian college, we had chapel services multiple times per week. But I didn't really pay attention to what mattered. I sang the words as they popped onto the screen, but my eyes wandered to the girls around me. I observed their bodies and compared them to mine.

Am I thinner than she is, or is she thinner than I am? I obsessed during chapel. *Are my hips wider? Is her stomach bigger? Are my arms smaller?*

The comparison game continued day after day after day. People turned into objects. Body parts turned into points on (or off) the scoreboard. Character qualities turned into players banished to the bench.

But chapel wasn't the only place where I played the comparison game. For example, I seriously envied my childhood friend, Erica.* She was a thin girl with thin legs and toned arms. Secretly, I hoped that I looked like her. I thought that maybe—just maybe—I did.

Until I realized that, in reality, Erica was skinny, and I wasn't.

The same was true of a college friend of mine named Ariel.** I looked at her—actually, studied her—and compared her body with mine. I pretended that we were practically the same size.

I could totally fit into her clothes, I thought confidently. *She might weigh a teeny bit less than me, but nothing significant. We're practically twins.*

Until I again realized that, in reality, Ariel was skinny, and I wasn't.

That was an insanely bitter pill for me to swallow. Ariel was the thinner friend in our relationship, and I was fooling myself to think that I was. I wanted to wear the size that she wore. I wanted to weigh what she weighed. I wanted to look as good in my clothes as she did.

As I nitpicked my flaws and the flaws of others, I failed to see people as people. I viewed them as objects that needed to be observed, critiqued, and

---

*   Name has been changed.
** Name has been changed.

compared. I should've been viewing them as human beings who needed to be loved, cared for, and encouraged. The comparison game was cruel and competitive. I had to fend for myself, just like everyone else on the field. May the skinniest girl win.

I didn't care how selfish or shallow it sounded—I wanted first prize.

real recovery expectation

I Will Accept How My New, Healthy Body Looks

By the way, that was the truth for my recovery, too. Even now, I have the desire to be skinny. But realistically, most females have that desire, whether they're ten years old or fifty years old.

I had to come to terms with the fact that my definition of the word "skinny" is my doctor's definition of the word "unhealthy." I also had to come to terms with the fact that some girls are simply thinner than I am. Sometimes, they're thinner because they have an eating disorder. Other times, they're thinner because God designed their bodies with different DNA than mine.

It's still difficult for me to hang out with girls who are thinner than I am. But that's not just a struggle for girls with eating disorders; it's a struggle for most (if not all) girls. It's simply a fact of life that I have to learn to accept. I'll probably never be the skinniest girl in the room, and I have to be okay with that.

I simply had to learn that my DNA is permanent. I can't transform it or make adjustments to it. But God gave me that DNA for a reason.

Today, I wouldn't describe myself as skinny. I wouldn't describe myself as fat either. I'm a healthy, young woman who is somewhere in between. Being in the middle has been an incredibly difficult reality for me to accept. But as I explained in chapter four, my body found its happy place when I began to accept that reality.

Honestly, a huge part of getting past anorexia—or any struggle in life—is to accept what you can't change. You can't transform your body. You can't modify your circumstances. You can't make the pain disappear. So accept that, even if it's artificial acceptance.

Artificial acceptance is the first step to genuine acceptance. Genuine acceptance may come later, but for now, learn to be "okay" when you really don't feel okay. You may always struggle to be around your friend who naturally has a fast metabolism, who adheres to a clean diet, or who is a workout rockstar. But you are your own worst critic. And your friend is her own worst critic, too.

Your friend who naturally has a fast metabolism is the worst critic of herself. Your friend who adheres to a clean diet is the worst critic of herself. And your friend who is a workout rockstar is the worst critic of herself.

It doesn't matter how beautiful a woman is. She still hates at least one thing about herself. I guarantee it. No woman—regardless of age, race, weight, height, eating disorder history, or anything else—is exempt from this.

Don't expect to magically stop being tempted to compare yourself to others during your eating disorder recovery. Instead, make the conscious choice *not to* compare yourself to others because of the negative consequences that result.

> Who is wise and understanding among you? By his good conduct let him show his works in the meekness of wisdom. But if you have bitter jealousy and selfish ambition in your hearts, do not boast and be false to the truth. This is not the wisdom that comes down from above, but is earthly, unspiritual, demonic. For where jealousy and selfish ambition exist, there will be disorder and every vile practice. But the wisdom from above is first pure, then peaceable, gentle, open to reason, full of mercy and good fruits, impartial and sincere. And a harvest of righteousness is sown in peace by those who make peace (James 3:13-18).

Real recovery looks like framing a photo of you with your friends—even if you're not the thinnest girl in the group—instead of hiding the photo away in a drawer. It looks like closing your eyes during church or class to avoid distractions instead of comparing yourself to every single girl in the room. It looks like choosing to use positive words to describe others—both in your mind and with your words—instead of objectifying people and their bodies. It looks like spending time with your naturally thin family members and friends—even if it's a little uncomfortable—instead of making excuses for why you don't have time for them. It looks like keeping your comments about your food intake, your exercise routine, and your size to yourself instead of "nonchalantly" discussing your healthy choices to make yourself look good.

After all, nonchalance might be more a more useful skill in sleuthing than in the comparison game.

false expectation

Guys Will Adore My New, Healthy Body

Although I don't know exactly what caused me to develop anorexia, I don't think my main motivation was to get a skinny body to attract lots of guys. That simply wasn't my upbringing. After all, I grew up in a conservative home and church, where I was taught about dressing modestly, letting guys take the lead in a relationship, and saving sex for marriage. I couldn't date until I was eighteen years old, so even though I wanted to have a boyfriend as an anorexic sixteen-year-old, I wasn't allowed to date.

I didn't mind that rule too much, especially because no guys seemed interested in me. Sure, I had crushes in middle school, high school, and beyond. But I had never dated or done the whole "I-like-you-and-you-like-me-but-we're-just-friends" thing.

As you've probably noticed, Ed likes to tell us single girls that we're still single because we're simply not beautiful enough. He deceives us into thinking that we'll get a boyfriend if we lose ten pounds, increase our daily workouts by fifteen minutes, or have toner legs. The funny thing about that is that if we continue to be single, Ed says that we need to lose ten *more* pounds, increase our daily workouts by fifteen *more* minutes, and have even *toner* legs. The endless cycle continues until we've either developed an eating disorder or given up on trying to meet Ed's endless demands. Hopefully, you'll always choose the second option, but it's hard to choose the second option when it feels like Ed might actually be right about the reason for your singleness.

After about two years of dealing with anorexia and six months of physical recovery, I started college with basically a new body. I hadn't been physically healthy in a long time, but I was relatively healthy as a college freshman. I attended a college that was ten hours from home, but I was roommates with my older sister, who kept an eye on me like good older sisters do.

I had all of the usual emotions about starting college out of state. I worried about making friends, wondered if I would have enough time for homework, and missed my family. And I thought that maybe, just maybe, my love life would be different than it had been at home.

After all, my little legs and my flat butt were things of the past. I finally had the long, blonde hair that I had been wanting for my entire life. My height and weight were finally in decent sync. I could still easily wear clothing from the juniors' department but moved on from the girls' department (for the most part).

However, despite my perfect size and shape, I still hated my body. My dad told me that I was beautiful, but I still didn't believe him. I especially doubted it when my first, second, third, and fourth years of college left me completely and utterly single. I had a major crush on Trent* throughout my four years of college, but I didn't want to pursue him. I wanted *him* to pursue *me*. After all, that sounded way more romantic. Except he didn't ask me out.

So, I hung out with my sister, my friends, and my Hulu shows. And they were good company on a Friday night or on a Saturday afternoon. But they didn't give me the affirmation that I craved—the affirmation that my new, healthy body was more beautiful than my old, sickly body. And I desperately wanted that affirmation from Trent. I wanted him to tell me that I was beautiful and thin and sexy.

---

*   Name has been changed.

This was how I saw it: if a guy chose me, he was choosing my heart *and* my body.

I wanted to hear from a guy's lips how my body made him crazy. From a guy who wanted to date me—not the size zero girl sitting next to him in the cafeteria. From a guy who wanted to marry me—not the girl with perfect abs in his history class. From a guy who wanted to have sex with me—not the girl beside him at the gym who looked like a supermodel in her sports bra and tiny shorts.

I mean, what if, when my future husband sees me completely naked for the very first time, he isn't enthralled by what he sees? What if he's disgusted by what he sees? Or worse, what if he's indifferent about what he sees?

On our wedding night, I'll take off all of my clothes in front of him. I won't be able to hide a single part of me from him. I won't be able to hide my thighs under a skirt or hide my stomach under a t-shirt or hide my arms in hoodie sleeves.

He'll see *all* of me. Every body part that disgusts me. Every wrinkle of skin that annoys me. Every flabby fold that I want to cover. He will see it. He will touch it. All of it will be his. But what if he secretly hates it?

I haven't actually had this nightmare, but I know exactly how it would go: it's the evening after my lovely wedding day, and I'm ready to make love with my new husband. As we walk into our honeymoon suite, we start to take off our clothes. For the first time, we're becoming naked in front of each other. We're ready to give ourselves to each other and become one.

My heart beats faster as I put on my lingerie for the first time. Like a little girl, I giggle excitedly and prance over to him across the room. I wait for him to smile his deep, thoughtful smile in response.

But instead of smiling, he frowns. Or—worse—a blank expression covers his face. Inside, I begin to panic. I feel like I can read his every thought. I assume that he hates my body and that it disgusts him—just like it disgusts me!

Rather than an exciting night of lovemaking, our exchange is cold and rigid. My new husband seems distant and distracted. He's quiet. I knew that he would hate my body, and now he's stuck with it forever. And I'm stuck with him hating it forever.

If you've ever had this nightmare (or daymare), know that it's likely from Ed. He wants you to doubt that you're beautiful and that any man could ever find your flawed body attractive. He wants you to crumple into a ball of self-pity and despair.

> But being crumpled into that ball isn't
> very smart—or comfortable.

real recovery expectation

The Right Guy Will Treasure My New, Healthy Body

To be honest, I didn't expect to be single at this point in my life. I expected to have been asked out multiple times or maybe even be engaged or married. After all, it felt like I knew many couples who had met in college. And as the years passed and I became a freshman, sophomore, junior, and senior in college, I started to feel quite abnormal.

Why had I never dated? Why wasn't I engaged? Would I ever get married? What was wrong with me?

I don't know what it's like to say yes or no when a guy invites me to go to dinner and a movie with him. I don't know what it's like to feel tingly as he reaches for my hand for the first time. I don't know what it's like to lean my head on his shoulder and hear him say that he loves me. I don't know what it's like to tell him about my craziest dreams, my scariest fears, or my biggest failures. I don't know what it's like to hear him say that I'm the most beautiful girl in the entire world, no matter how ugly I think I am.

I can blame my lack of these experiences on my body. I can believe Ed's lies that my body is simply too fat or not toned enough or uber ugly. I can promise to eat even less than I already eat and exercise even more than I already exercise. But those aren't the reasons that I don't have a long line of guys waiting at my doorstep.

Finding love is simply a matter of time, not a matter of size.

I truly believe that God has wired every man to be attracted to a certain kind of woman. After all, why did Adam love Eve? Why did Abraham love Sarah? Why did Isaac love Rebekah? I personally think that it's because God designed them to be physically attracted to each other's bodies.

Obviously, God didn't promise that I'll get married. He never said that I'll meet a guy who'll fall in love with me and adore my body. And He never guaranteed that I would meet Prince Charming by my college graduation. But I believe that if it's God's will, I'll get married to a man who truly loves me and every single part of my broken body.

Here's the evidence that I have for that statement—all kinds of people get married. Underweight, overweight, tall, short, light-haired, dark-haired, no-haired, blue-eyed, brown-eyed, green-eyed, and the list goes on. It's not just the women who wear a size zero, the women who have toned thighs, or the women who have a flat stomach who find love.

And just to let you know, if a guy simply wants you for your body, then he doesn't deserve you. That may sound haughty, but it's true. A guy who truly loves you will love your body *and* your heart.

As long as it's God's will for me to get married, then a great guy is going to want my body. He'll think that it's sexy, even if I won't. He'll someday tell me that I'm gorgeous. I'll finally get the affirmation that I wanted from Trent for way too many years of my life.

Interestingly, it doesn't sound like Solomon's lover, the Shulamite woman, was stick-thin. It doesn't sound like she was a little, sickly girl. Her feet, hips, stomach, breasts, neck, eyes, nose, head, and height are all mentioned in the passage below. But they're not described as small or skinny. And Solomon thought that she was so wonderful that he married her. In fact, he viewed her body as beautiful.

Others

Return, return, O Shulammite, return, return, that we may look upon you.

He

Why should you look upon the Shulammite, as upon a dance before two armies? How beautiful are your feet in sandals, O noble daughter! Your rounded thighs are like jewels, the work of a master hand. Your navel is a rounded bowl that never lacks mixed wine. Your belly is a heap of wheat, encircled with lilies. Your two breasts are like two fawns, twins of a gazelle. Your neck is like an ivory tower. Your eyes are pools in Heshbon, by the gate of Bath-rabbim. Your nose is like a tower of Lebanon, which looks toward Damascus. Your head crowns you like Carmel, and your flowing locks are like purple; a king is held captive in the tresses. How beautiful and pleasant you are, O loved one, with all your delights! Your stature is like a palm tree, and your breasts are like its clusters. I say I will climb the palm tree and lay hold of its fruit. Oh may your breasts be like clusters of the vine, and the scent of your breath like apples, and your mouth like the best wine.

She

It goes down smoothly for my beloved, gliding over lips and teeth. I am my beloved's, and his desire is for me (Song of Songs 6:13-7:10).

Real recovery looks like wearing clothes that fully cover your private areas instead of relying on your low-cut, tight, or short clothing to get the attention that you crave. It looks like waiting patiently for the right guy to make a move instead of asking guys out because you doubt that anyone will actually find you beautiful enough to ask. It looks like trusting that God wants the best for your love life instead of assuming that you're still single because you're fat and ugly. It looks like maintaining your physical and emotional boundaries instead of falling for whoever comments on your "hot" body. It looks like having enough dignity and self-worth to accept a genuine compliment about your body from a well-intentioned guy instead of shying away from any and every genuine compliment that you receive.

After all, confidence is sexy, too.

false expectation

God Will Help Me Recover Quickly

Ed was like the controlling boyfriend everyone always told me to avoid but to whom I was always drawn. For some reason, I was attracted to him. He intrigued me. He made me an offer that I couldn't refuse, and I fell for it.

"If you do whatever I tell you to do, I'll give you a skinny body," Ed promised me.

So, I did.

I didn't sign a legal document to make our relationship official. In fact, our relationship formed quite discreetly and continued quite gradually. I didn't want anyone to know that I had decided to be with such a controlling "boyfriend." And Ed told me that our relationship had to be kept secret. No one was to know.

Days turned into weeks. Weeks turned into months. Months turned into years. And Ed consumed more and more of my time and energy. He certainly filled most of my thoughts.

Whatever he told me, I naïvely believed. Whatever he said to do, I submissively obeyed. Whatever he wanted from me, I willingly gave him.

I looked to Ed to fulfill my needs and my desires. I ran to him over and over again, clinging to him. Still, he never provided the affirmation that I longed for or the comfort that I craved. He was *always* unsatisfied with me. I felt like I would never be able to please him.

When I lost five pounds, he said, "Just lose five more pounds, okay?" When I fit into a tiny size, he whispered, "You can fit into the even smaller size if you try." When I thought that I was finally skinnier than her, he told me, "But you're not skinnier than that *other* girl."

Ed never told me that I was skinny. He never said that I was beautiful. He never said that I was enough. Eventually, I did try to break up with Ed, but I couldn't stay away from him. Even though I knew that he was a loser, I still clung to him with all of my might. He refused to let me go, but I was somehow okay with that because *I* refused to let *him* go.

Everyone told me what an evil liar he was, but I ignored them. I believed Ed over the people who loved and cared about me. Instead of trusting my family, my doctors, and my counselors, I trusted the liar. I said that I would give more attention to God's truth and less attention to Ed's lies. But he kept beckoning me to come back to him. So, I went back to him—even though he made me feel like a toad instead of a princess.

To be honest, when I was struggling with anorexia and recovery, I was a bad Christian girl trying to be a good Christian girl. Sure, I was a pro at looking like a good Christian girl on the outside. I read the Bible, prayed, and listened to Christian music. I dressed up on Sunday mornings, attended Sunday school and youth group, and carried on conversations with visitors at church. I blogged about the Bible, talked about theology, and memorized Scripture verses. I served in Awana, led a Bible study, and volunteered for Vacation Bible School.

But if you had seen the real me—deep down inside where only God could see—you would've seen all of the rubbish in my heart. You would've seen my desperation, my self-obsession, and my control issues. You would've seen my deception and pride. You would've seen my many idols and certainly my biggest idol—Ed. You would've seen that nothing really mattered to me besides my body.

My relationship with God was all an act. I was going through the motions because I was living for myself while acting like I was living for God. I was reaching out to God with one hand but clinging to Ed with the other.

I had become a Christian when I was a young child, but I definitely wasn't living like a Christian. I didn't really love God. If I had truly loved Him, then I would've kept His commandments (John 14:15, 21). I wouldn't have shared my worship between Him and Ed. I wouldn't have lied to my family about *everything*.

Everything that I thought, said, and did as an anorexic (and even during my recovery) was deceptive. My goal was to get away with eating as few calories as possible while burning as many calories as possible. I felt the Holy Spirit's conviction, but Ed told me to ignore it. So, I listened to Ed and ignored the Holy Spirit.

You had to look past my stack of devotionals, church clothes, Bible knowledge, and service hours to see the real me. But the real me was there.

I just didn't want to *show* the real me because
it meant that I would have to leave Ed behind.

real recovery expectation
God Will Help Me Recover in His Timing

Honestly, the only thing that kept me from losing more weight than I had already lost was my parents' intervention. Because I was so secretive about my anorexic habits and was losing weight pretty gradually, my parents didn't seriously intervene until I had been struggling with anorexia for a couple of years. They worried about my health, diet, and exercise routine. I did start seeing a counselor, who tried to encourage me to eat better. But I didn't eat better, so nothing really changed.

My parents continued to worry about my health. At the recommendation of my counselor, my mom scheduled an appointment for me with a nutritionist at our local hospital. You know what happened next—the worst day of my life.

The next six months were pure torture for me. I despised the precise meal chart and exercise restrictions that my nutritionist had placed on me. That period of recovery was mostly physical. Everyone's goal—except mine, of course—was to make sure that I reached a healthy weight.

But then there was a period of mostly mental, emotional, and spiritual recovery. I was at the hospital, at the doctor's office, and in counseling sessions quite frequently. I saw two different general practitioners, a nutritionist, three different counselors, and an eating disorder specialist during that period.

And that period of recovery has lasted for several years. Honestly, my recovery has lasted *much* longer than my actual eating disorder did. I have a hunch that my recovery wouldn't have lasted so long if I had had realistic expectations about my recovery in the first place.

I expected that God would somehow fix everything with which I was struggling—my distorted body image, my incorrect thoughts, my mixed-up priorities, and even my actual body.

Here are some of the prayer requests that I prayed for during my recovery journey:

- "Help me learn to accept my body and actively fight the lies."
- "Help me accept Your timing and Your will about my recovery and my body."
- "Help Ed go away forever and soon."
- "Help me lose five pounds." (Yes, that really was one of my prayer requests and sometimes still is.)

Nothing was inherently wrong with those prayer requests (except maybe the last one, ahem). But they were a bit general and even a bit misguided perhaps. For example, Ed (also known as Satan) isn't going away until he's "thrown into the lake of fire and sulfur" (Rev. 20:10). He's always prowling around for a victim (1 Peter 5:8).

My thoughts on common Scriptures were somewhat misguided as well. Typically, Psalm 139:13-14 is the passage that people use in their attempts to help young women who are recovering from an eating disorder. They definitely mean well in referring to this passage, and it *is* the truth because it's from God's Word. But because my focus was on being thin and not on being "wonderfully made," the passage didn't comfort me.

A while ago, I actually wrote something specifically about this passage: "I'm sick of hearing Psalm 139:13-14. It's a Band-Aid that people slap on an eating disorder and hope sticks. But it doesn't stick on me. The passage doesn't tell me that I'm thin or attractive or even beautiful."

Perhaps you can relate to my frustration with the frequent usage of this passage. Or perhaps you've heard 1 Samuel 16:7, 1 Timothy 2:9-10, or 1 Peter 3:3-4 mentioned instead. Sometimes, Bible verses are used like Band-Aids to slap on our souls instead of as tools to help us grow in our understanding of God.

Needless to say, during my recovery journey, I had pretty unrealistic expectations about the power of prayer and the Bible. In viewing them as a magic potion, I definitely overestimated them. However, I underestimated how God would use them—and a million other things—to gradually guide me in my recovery journey.

He used my parents, my sisters, my extended family members, and my friends to speak the truth to me about who I was—both on the inside and on the outside. He used my counselors to teach me ways to deal with my negative thoughts. He used my doctors to provide objective facts about my weight and health. He even used a stranger in a restaurant to remind me how He had rescued me.

It happened on a typical Sunday during my recovery from anorexia. I was sitting in church and thinking about my still-disordered eating and my still-required food for the day—as was my custom. And I felt greatly discouraged—as was also my custom. A wave of depression overcame me as I sat there in silence.

After church, my family and I went out to eat. But to be honest, I was distracted for most of our lunch because a severely anorexic girl was escorted to her table just minutes before my family was. Her family sat in the booth across from ours. I realized that our timing and seating arrangement weren't coincidental. God knew that I needed to see her.

The girl's legs looked like twigs. Her teeny jeans hung loosely on her legs. Her eyes sagged, and her hands shook as she brought her fork to her mouth. She didn't smile. She was sullen and silent as she rested her head on the table. Her parents had to hold her up as she walked to and from the table because she couldn't manage to walk the short distance by herself.

To this day, thinking about that encounter makes me feel sick inside.

Of course, that girl wasn't beyond recovery. She could've found help at any moment. Healing was a possibility for her, even in her severely anorexic state. But I think that God placed her in my journey through recovery to show me that He was listening to my prayers and working in my struggles.

Truth be told, I believed that *I* was the reason that I had physically recovered from anorexia. After all, *I* was the one who ate the food groups on my meal chart. *I* was the one who reduced my exercise. *I* was the one who regularly visited the nutritionist. *I* was the one who regained the weight. *I* was the one who heard Ed's excruciatingly painful lies over and over again in my mind.

I figured that since I had been the reason that I had recovered physically from anorexia, I would have to be the reason that I recovered emotionally, mentally, and spiritually from anorexia as well. From my flawed perspective, God wasn't helping me recover from anorexia. I was recovering through sheer will-power and determination, so I deserved the admiration for my efforts thus far and for my future efforts.

But what I didn't want to admit was that I had been a few mere pounds away from being the skeletally thin girl in the restaurant. If I had continued journeying through anorexia—on the path of "just a few more pounds to lose"—then I would've been in the same exact place as that girl. Resting my head on the table. Shaking as I ate. Stumbling out the door.

But in God's kindness toward me, He gave me the courage that I needed to choose recovery.

At the restaurant on that Sunday afternoon, we had to wait an *hour* for our meal. It wasn't fun to wait that long. But every minute of the wait was worth it because I had been begging God for help as I struggled with my recovery, and I finally felt like maybe He was really listening to my prayers—the ones that seemed to bounce off the ceiling and onto my lap, the ones that I begrudgingly prayed to check off my quiet time to-do list, and the ones that I prayed in apathy and even disbelief.

God didn't help me recover from anorexia using Scripture, prayer, people, and events because I deserved His help. He helped me recover from anorexia because He is kind, compassionate, and faithful.

> ["]Upon her children also I will have no mercy, because they are children of whoredom. For their mother has played the whore; she who conceived them has acted shamefully. For she said, 'I will go after my lovers, who give me my bread and my water, my wool and my flax, my oil and my drink.' Therefore I will hedge up her way with thorns, and I will build a wall against her, so that she cannot find her paths. She shall pursue her lovers but not overtake them, and she shall seek them but shall not find them. Then she shall say, 'I will go and return to my first husband, for it was better for me then than now.' And she did not know that it was I who gave her the grain, the wine, and the oil, and who lavished on her silver and gold, which they used for Baal. Therefore I will take back my grain in its time, and my wine in its season, and I will take away my wool and my flax, which were to cover her nakedness. Now I will uncover her lewdness in the sight of her lovers, and no one shall rescue her out of my hand. And I will put an end to all her mirth, her feasts, her new moons, her Sabbaths, and all her appointed feasts. And I will lay waste her vines and her fig trees, of which she said, 'These are my wages, which my lovers have given me.' I will make them a forest, and the beasts of the field shall devour them. And I will punish her for the feast days of the Baals when she burned offerings to them and adorned herself with her ring and jewelry, and went after her lovers and forgot me, declares the LORD.

> "Therefore, behold, I will allure her, and bring her into the wilderness, and speak tenderly to her. And there I will give her her vineyards and make the Valley of Achor a door of hope. And there she shall answer as in the days of her youth, as at the time when she came out of the land of Egypt.

"And in that day, declares the LORD, you will call me 'My Husband,' and no longer will you call me 'My Baal.' For I will remove the names of the Baals from her mouth, and they shall be remembered by name no more. And I will make for them a covenant on that day with the beasts of the field, the birds of the heavens, and the creeping things of the ground. And I will abolish the bow, the sword, and war from the land, and I will make you lie down in safety. And I will betroth you to me forever. I will betroth you to me in righteousness and in justice, in steadfast love and in mercy. I will betroth you to me in faithfulness. And you shall know the LORD["] (Hosea 2:4-20).

Real recovery looks like being alert to the ways that God is using the Bible, prayer, people, and events to help you recover instead of turning a blind eye to the ways that He is working. It looks like writing and frequently repeating a breakup song or speech for Ed instead of running back to him whenever he beckons. It looks like acknowledging the progress that God has made in your recovery journey so far instead of complaining that He hasn't been helping you or declaring that you deserve the praise for your progress. It looks like asking God for specific things in your recovery, such as peace about your weight or a counselor who understands your situation, instead of praying super general prayers and expecting to see results easily. It looks like committing to read the Bible and pray daily no matter how you feel instead of claiming that it doesn't matter whether you spend time with God or not.

After all, that's exactly what Ed used to tell me, but I think he's a bit biased.

false expectation
I Will Lose My Desire to Control

Ed *really* didn't want to let me go.

He desperately wanted me to stay in the dark where no one could help me find freedom from him. His grip on me was unbelievably tight, and he hated when I eventually chose recovery. I can still feel his grip on me now, even as a "recovered" anorexic.

When my parents found out that I had been living so unhealthily, they connected me with a counselor, who connected me with a nutritionist, who connected me with a cardiologist . . . and the list continued.

Ed was furious, and I was terrified. All of a sudden, I could no longer be in charge of the food that I ate or the exercise that I did. My every move was analyzed by my family members so that I would stick to the plan that my nutritionist had made for me to regain the weight that I had lost. My life felt out of control.

Once I had regained the weight that I had lost, my actions still had to be closely monitored. I still had to follow specific rules about my food and exercise to ensure that I didn't lose any weight or resume my dangerous habits. My general practitioner still wanted my period to happen regularly. My nutritionist still wanted to see me frequently. My counselor still wanted to chat about how I was progressing. My life *still* felt out of control.

I wrote this on the day after I deleted the step tracker app on my phone: "Believe it or not, that was one of the hardest things that I've ever done. Now I can't track how many calories I burn or how many steps I walk. I'm scared to death that I'm going to gain weight and fat and hate my body even more . . . I won't burn enough calories to make up for the calories that I'm required to eat. And that makes me terrified."

From my perspective, stepping on the scale was scarier than skydiving out of an airplane. Eating fettuccine Alfredo, Chinese food, or a milkshake was a worse sin than robbing a bank. Buying the next size up was more agonizing than watching live surgery. Having a meal in an unknown place with an unknown caloric content was more dreadful than taking the SAT in a random classroom full of strangers. Not being able to do my workout at the exact hour and for the exact amount of time that I had planned was more nerve-wracking than having to *retake* the SAT in *another* random classroom full of strangers.

Obviously, I had a plethora of fears during my anorexia journey and my recovery journey. (Those were just a few of them!) Ed used fear to influence me to stay with him. He said that as long as I did what he told me to do, I had no reason to fear. I could control how I looked, even if I couldn't control anything else in my life.

I also had a plethora of arbitrary rules to correspond with my plethora of fears. For example, when I was discussing with my general practitioner how much I should weigh, I had a very specific weight in mind that I wanted to maintain and feared exceeding—even if I didn't have a regular menstrual period, still had flaky nails, or still looked like a pale ghost at that weight.

Likewise, when I started having a minimum daily caloric requirement to meet instead of having food group boxes on a meal chart to check off, I had a very specific number of calories that I wanted to eat and feared exceeding. It didn't matter to me if I didn't feel satisfied after eating those calories, got painful headaches from not eating enough, or didn't eat for extended periods of time.

Along the same lines, keeping a pillow over my stomach while I sat on the couch made me feel less self-conscious. Wearing my coat around the house— even when I was burning up—made me feel less fat. Behind that pillow and underneath that coat was a stomach that I despised. There was no logical reason for me to despise it, but I did anyway.

I still do very arbitrary things that please Ed but exhaust me. There's still an arbitrary weight, caloric intake, exercise routine, and clothing size that I worry about not maintaining. Having these self-imposed limits makes me feel safe. Comfortable. In control. But there's a great irony in all of my efforts to be in control. While I believe that I'm in control, Ed is actually the one in control of me.

He uses me to gain that control—when I let him.

real recovery expectation
I Will Better Manage My Desire to Control

At some point during my recovery, I realized that the key to recovering from an eating disorder is simply overcoming fear. Of course, I can't speak to every fear that you've had during your eating disorder experience. But I firmly believe that fear is the reason that eating disorders develop and that fear is the reason that eating disorders continue.

Perhaps I should be more specific, though. I'm portraying fear in a very negative light, but in reality, fear isn't problematic *unless you give into it*. I firmly believe that *giving into fear* is the reason that eating disorders develop and that *giving into fear* is the reason that eating disorders continue.

Recovering from your eating disorder doesn't mean that you'll suddenly have fewer negative emotions (including fear). Honestly, your negative emotions will never go away on this earth. Rather, when you decide that you want to recover from your eating disorder, you're making the decision to give into your fear less often.

You're no longer freaking out when you can't comfortably fit in your favorite pair of anorexia-era jeans. You don't obsess about how many calories were in your breakfast. You're not brooding if your weight increases by a single pound. You don't feel depressed if you don't have time for a workout after school. You're not despairing if your grandma makes creamy chicken pot pie for dinner instead of low-cal vegetable soup. You don't befriend or neglect someone based on his or her size.

As I discussed in chapter six, one of the biggest fears that I had as a recovering anorexic was that I wouldn't be skinny anymore. I was willing to pay any price to be considered "thin" by my family, friends, and complete strangers. I didn't want to be "average" or "in the middle." I didn't even want to be healthy.

Now, with a couple years of experience, I've learned that life isn't so bad here in the middle. It's not as terrifying as Ed made it out to be. And being in the middle won't be as terrifying for you either.

Of course, I know how much Ed hates that I'm sharing all of this with you. Even though I still struggle to accept my body, I don't struggle as much as I used to. And he doesn't want you to find the freedom that I've begun to find.

The first thing that I ever wrote and published about my struggle with anorexia was a post that focused on body image. I didn't go into detail about my personal body image, eating disorder, or recovery. In fact, I didn't even directly say that I was recovering from anorexia. But sharing this post helped me take a small step toward recovery.

Similarly, when I was a junior in college, my discipleship group leader invited me and her other group members to share our testimonies via video chat. I decided that it was time to be real about my eating disorder. On that night, I shared a lot of details about my eating disorder that I didn't normally share with my friends. Before then, I hadn't brought it up with many people, but I'm glad that I did that night.

And when I told the girls in my discipleship group the truth, their jaws didn't drop in shock. They didn't start bawling or moaning. Rather, they listened quietly with grace and kindness. My deep, dark secret was no longer a secret from them.

Recently, I gave a guest lecture—my first guest lecture ever—in a college psychology class at my alma mater. I purposely discussed the topic of eating disorders and how my anorexia had affected me. In fact, anorexia was the focus of my discussion. I knew some of the students in that classroom; others didn't look familiar. But I didn't care because I had a message to share: people who are struggling with an eating disorder aren't doing well physically, mentally, emotionally, or spiritually—and we need to learn to understand them so that we can help them.

Now, people actually know that I had an eating disorder. In fact, while this book was still a disorganized jumble of words, I wanted people to know that I was writing it. Now that it's an actual organized and coherent story, I want people to read it.

During high school and even part of college, my friends didn't know that I tracked every calorie that I consumed. They didn't know that the reason that I didn't want to hang out with them in the afternoon was because I exercised in the afternoon. They didn't know that their birthday parties stressed me out because I had to eat their calorie-laden cupcakes. They didn't know how much I loathed my stomach, hips, or arms. They didn't know that I had to see a nutritionist, a cardiologist, and an eating disorder specialist.

People finding out about my journey through anorexia and my journey through recovery was a positive thing. With every person who discovered the truth about my struggle, Ed lost some of his control over me. And I received their support and encouragement.

Since publishing my first post about body image, I've published many more—not just about body image but also about eating disorders and recovery. I've written about the challenges that accompany swimsuit season, the lies Ed whispers to vulnerable young women, and the myth that women should love their bodies. And guess what I picked as one of the main topics when I led a discipleship group during my senior year of college? Identifying Satan's lies and combating them with the truth.

Telling other people about your eating disorder can help you have a better recovery. Being honest about your past—and your present—is an important step in your recovery journey. Even though Ed wants you to keep your mouth shut so that you'll continue to live in fear, you don't have to stay silent any longer. You *can* tell, and you *should* tell. You never know who'll be able to offer you helpful advice, encouragement, and care during your battle. And you never know who'll appreciate your transparency and relate to your story.

Another way to help you lose your desire for control is to accept your recovery timeline—especially your mental, emotional, and spiritual recovery timeline. You may be able to accelerate your physical recovery with a particular meal plan or exercise routine or medication. But your mental, emotional, and spiritual recovery may feel completely out of your control because you can't accelerate things like acceptance, belief, and confidence.

For me, recovering from anorexia was *not* a flip-the-switch kind of process. My recovery journey took much longer than I had anticipated, which left me feeling disgruntled and discouraged. Not only is patience crucial for recovery, but perseverance is also.

When I saw an eating disorder specialist at Children's National Hospital, he told me that there are three different groups of eating disorder patients. The people in the first group never recover from their eating disorders and are trapped in the eating disorder cycle for life. The people in the second group are able to move on from their eating disorders, though they may always struggle. The people in the third group completely recover from their eating disorders and basically forget about them.

My eating disorder specialist explained that about one-third of individuals recovering from an eating disorder fall into each group. That, of course, made me wonder in which group I would fall. After all, I had about a thirty percent chance of winding up in any of those groups.

It has been several years since my eating disorder specialist shared that information with me. For now, I've decided that I fall into the second group. And I may stay in that group forever—who knows? With that realization, I have to learn to be okay with being in the second group. I may always struggle with anorexic tendencies, and I have to accept that.

I don't know which group you fall into—the first group of constant struggle, the second group of moderate struggle, or the third group of forgotten struggle. Of course, I hope that you fall into the third group and that your eating disorder becomes a distant memory. But even if you don't fall into the third group, know that the only way that Ed will take control of your life again is if you let him—if you give into the lies that he introduces, the doubts that he plants in your mind, and the fears with which he taunts you.

It's true that there are a lot of things that are out of your control, especially with your eating disorder recovery. I totally get that. But you can control what you choose to believe and whom you choose to believe.

> Let no one deceive you with empty words, for because of these things the wrath of God comes upon the sons of disobedience. Therefore do not become partners with them; for at one time you were darkness, but now you are light in the Lord. Walk as children of light (for the fruit of light is found in all that is good and right and true), and try to discern what is pleasing to the Lord. Take no part in the unfruitful works of darkness, but instead expose them. For it is shameful even to speak of the things that they do in secret. But when anything is exposed by the light, it becomes visible, for anything that becomes visible is light (Eph. 5:6-14).

Real recovery looks like finding something that you can control besides your weight—like your weekend itinerary, your route to work, or your bedroom décor—instead of always trying to control your weight when life feels out of control. It looks like opening up about your eating disorder journey with a Christian you trust instead of keeping it hidden from everyone. It looks like loosening your grip on the one thing that you've determinedly tried to control—like an arbitrary weight, size, caloric intake, or workout routine—instead of retaining your grip on that one thing. It looks like sharing transparently about your eating disorder in order to encourage others who have an eating disorder instead of refusing to mention your past and current struggles. It looks like giving up control of your life to God instead of refusing to let God have control.

> After all, God is already in control, and your emotional rollercoaster has a better chance of staying on the track when you realize that.

false expectation

Recovery Will Make Me All Better

I just ate a bowl of sugary cereal. With one percent milk instead of skim milk. At 12:30 a.m. Right before I headed to bed. But when Ed started to scold me, I tuned him out.

Earlier today (before my midnight snack), I ate a Pop-Tart. And a brownie. And a cookie. But when Ed started to scold me, I tuned him out.

Believe it or not, Ed still speaks to me quite often, even though anorexia has been in my rearview mirror for years. He still tells me what to eat, what not to eat, how much to eat, how much not to eat, when to eat, when not to eat, how to exercise, how long to exercise, how often to exercise...and the list never ends.

When I started to recover from anorexia, Ed's voice still seemed very loud. He continued to invade my mind long after I had reached a healthy weight again. He continued to make me feel guilty for my actions that didn't align with his plans for me.

But I just wanted to be *fixed*. I wanted to not have such awful thoughts about myself or such a strong hatred for my reflection in the mirror. I wanted to not have such intense anxiety about the number on the scale, such intense guilt about the food that I ate, or such intense shame about the exercise that I *didn't* do.

Still, no matter how many books I read, no matter how many songs I listened to, no matter how many counseling appointments I had, no matter how many compliments I received, no matter how many blog posts I read, no matter how many clever quotes I saw, no matter how many dosage changes to my anxiety medication I made, no matter how many sermons I heard, and no matter how many Bible verses I read, I didn't feel fixed.

At some point very late in my recovery journey, I started to realize that *none* of those things would fix me. To be honest, I felt like even God wouldn't fix me. If I wanted to be fixed, I thought that I would have to fix myself.

But despite my naïve and persistent longing that something—*anything*—would fix me, nothing did. The books that I read were depressing. The songs that I listened to felt fake. The counseling appointments that I had seemed repetitive. The compliments that I received felt shallow. The blog posts that I read were unhelpful. The clever quotes that I saw seemed cliché. The dosage changes to my anxiety medication felt pointless. The sermons that I heard were too convicting. The Bible verses that I read seemed overused.

Truth be told, I didn't really want to be "all better" from my anorexia. I still wanted to have an unhealthily low BMI. I still wanted to buy clothing from the girls' department. I still wanted to eat salads whenever I went out to dinner. I still wanted to skip my periods. I still wanted to eat one-hundred-calorie breakfasts every day. But if I still did all of those things, I wouldn't be writing this book. By the grace of God, I dipped my toe into the pool of freedom.

I made progress, and I found real recovery.

real recovery expectation

Recovery Will Be Possible

I believe that real recovery—in every sense of the phrase—means taking a single step toward progress. Then another step. Then another step. And countless more steps.

The misconception that I had about my recovery from anorexia was that my bad thoughts about my body and my fears about eating and exercise would disappear into thin air. But they didn't. And they still haven't.

I'm still disgusted by my size. I still loathe my weight. I still hate my stomach, hips, butt, thighs, and arms. From an objective standpoint, I'm physically healthy. I'm actually thin. There's no logical reason for me to feel this way about myself. But I can eat in a healthy way and exercise in a healthy way *despite* my disgust, loathing, and hatred.

Real recovery means defying Ed—one lie at a time. So, order those loaded nachos when you go out with your friends. Skip a workout after a long day at work. Stop weighing yourself every morning. Set up an appointment with a Christian counselor. Toss your favorite diet cookbook in the trash. Wear the dress that everyone says makes you look beautiful. Read Scriptures that speak the truth about your identity and believe that those words apply to you. Defy Ed and keep defying Ed and never stop defying Ed.

Real recovery is the place where calories—whether on your plate, on your lunch's nutrition label, or on your treadmill screen—aren't the center of your life. It's the place where eating isn't as scary and where exercise isn't as necessary. It's the place where buying the next size up isn't shameful and where getting rid of old clothes isn't unbearable. It's the place where going out to dinner isn't so stressful and where eating dessert isn't such a crime. It's the place where tracking calories is more of a chore and where counting steps is less of a compulsion. It's the place where gaining a couple pounds isn't the worst thing ever and where losing a couple pounds isn't the best thing ever.

Real recovery may require you to take the medication that you've always avoided or to stop taking the medication in which you've always indulged. It may require you to stay in the hospital or the recovery facility that terrifies you or to stop staying in the hospital or recovery facility where you've grown comfortable. It may require you to admit that you have depression, anxiety, or obsessive-compulsive disorder or to stop using those things as an excuse. It may require you to see the doctor about whom you've heard horror stories or to stop seeing the doctor whom you've loved since childhood.

Real recovery means that you have the energy to go to work, do well in school, and take care of the people you love. It means that you have the oomph to get out of bed in the morning, push your little sister on the swing, and take a walk with your friends. It means that your bones are strong instead of constantly breaking. It means that your nails are growing instead of flaking. It means that you aren't freezing in the July heat. It means that you can breathe without difficulty. It means that you have a period every month.

Based on how my recovery happened, you'll experience real recovery when your body matters less to you than it did before. But your body will (most likely) still matter to you. After all, when I was younger, I noticed the things that I disliked about myself. For example, I disliked my flat hair and dry hands. However, I wasn't consumed by the aspects of my body that I disliked. I was *aware* of them but not *obsessed* about them. They didn't make me crazy or cause me to take any drastic actions to fix them. I used a curling iron to make my flat hair curly, and I used lotion to make my chapped hands smoother. But I didn't have surgery, buy a five-hundred-dollar hand cream, or even get a perm.

Now, post-anorexia, I don't expect to love my body. And you shouldn't expect to love your body either. You may never love your body—but that's okay. If you're waiting to love your body so that you can consider yourself "recovered" from your eating disorder, you may be waiting a lifetime. Unfortunately, *not* loving your body is a part of womanhood.

But if you can observe without obsessing, you're recovering. That means observing nutrition labels without obsessing about them, observing your weight on the scale without obsessing about it, observing others in your workout class without obsessing about them, and observing size charts without obsessing about them.

Real recovery doesn't start with a lightbulb moment of realization or a magic formula that changes how you view your body. Real recovery doesn't start when you see yourself as stunning or thin or attractive or when you feel "all better." Real recovery is when you make your first step toward progress.

> For those who live according to the flesh set their minds on the things of the flesh, but those who live according to the Spirit set their minds on the things of the Spirit. For to set the mind on the flesh is death, but to set the mind on the Spirit is life and peace. For the mind that is set on the flesh is hostile to God, for it does not submit to God's law; indeed, it cannot. Those who are in the flesh cannot please God. You, however, are not in the flesh but in the Spirit, if in fact the Spirit of God dwells in you. Anyone who does not have the Spirit of Christ does not belong to him. But if Christ is in you, although the body is dead because of sin, the Spirit is life because of righteousness. If the Spirit of him who raised Jesus from the dead dwells in you, he who raised Christ Jesus from the dead will also give life to your mortal bodies through his Spirit who dwells in you. So then, brothers, we are debtors, not to the flesh, to live according to

the flesh. For if you live according to the flesh you will die, but if by the Spirit you put to death the deeds of the body, you will live. For all who are led by the Spirit of God are sons of God. For you did not receive the spirit of slavery to fall back into fear, but you have received the Spirit of adoption as sons, by whom we cry, "Abba! Father!" The Spirit himself bears witness with our spirit that we are children of God, and if children, then heirs—heirs of God and fellow heirs with Christ, provided we suffer with him in order that we may also be glorified with him. For I consider that the sufferings of this present time are not worth comparing with the glory that is to be revealed to us (Rom. 8:5-18).

Real recovery looks like understanding that every kind of recovery has value—whether it's physical, mental, emotional, or spiritual—instead of believing that only specific kinds of recovery have value. It looks like choosing to make baby steps in the right direction instead of expecting yourself to make giant leaps in the right direction. It looks like getting up off the ground when Ed or anyone else pushes you down instead of staying stuck on the ground. It looks like thanking God for the courage that He has given you to recover instead of despairing that you don't have enough strength to recover. It looks like believing the truth that your recovery is possible instead of giving into the lie that your recovery is impossible.

**After all, real recovery is possible
because you *are* recovering!**

Afterword
How to Help Someone You Know Who Has an Eating Disorder

Before, during, and after I was recovering from anorexia, I knew several people who had an eating disorder. At least, I thought that they did; it can be difficult to know for sure. But I didn't really know how to help them find recovery from their eating disorders. It's even harder for individuals who have never had an eating disorder know how to help others find recovery from theirs, besides offering prayers and kind words to them.

Watching someone you love suffer for any reason is incredibly hard—whether that someone has chronic pain, loses a job, experiences a breakup, undergoes abuse, or has an eating disorder. But watching someone you love *move on* from suffering is perhaps harder—whether that someone seeks to find a cure from the chronic pain, searches for a new job, rebounds from the broken relationship, heals from the abuse, or recuperates from the eating disorder—because you don't know how to help them journey through recovery.

That's why I wanted my parents and sisters to share their thoughts with you about my recovery.

Chris McCready (Dad)

As I tried to explain to Grace the cardiologist's concern for the potential heart issues resulting from her anorexia, my angel daughter—who had always been so engaging, silly, and full of life—stared right through me with no hint of emotion or concern. My wife and I lined up counselors, doctors, and a nutritionist to help Grace in her recovery. The roots of the lie that Satan had told her were unimaginably deep. We just wanted our daughter back. So, we "pray[ed] without ceasing" (1 Thess. 5:17).

God was merciful and answered our prayers. He never gave up on Grace or on us, despite our weaknesses. Her recovery didn't happen quickly, but it happened steadily. God restored her health, her fun-loving personality, and even her silliness.

Father, thank You for Your mercy toward us and toward our daughter. Thank You for freeing her from the dark prison of Satan's lies, shame, and deception. As David wrote, "I believe that I shall look upon the goodness of the LORD in the land of the living!" (Psalm 27:13).

Jennifer McCready (Mom)

In the gospel of John, Jesus told His disciples, "'And you will know the truth, and the truth will set you free'" (John 8:32). During Grace's recovery, she needed to hear the truth. She needed us to tell her the truth, and she needed to hear the truth from others. She needed to be told the truth again and again and again.

I, too, needed to hear the truth. And the truth that I needed to hear was this: "I believe that I shall look upon the goodness of the Lord in the land of the living!" (Psalm 27:13). I did despair, but God is so good. I've seen His goodness in healing Grace.

Anna McCready (Big Sis)

Although I was away at college for most of Grace's eating disorder, I was there during her recovery process. It was hard to see my sweet, cheerful sister so far removed from herself, and at times, it was difficult for us to get along.

However, God worked through our parents, her counselors, her doctors, and her own recovery efforts to pull her out of the pit. And, as a result, she's now more herself than ever. Praise God!

Jenna McCready (Little Sis)

I remember the day that I overheard the doctor first use the word "anorexia" to describe Grace's condition, and I was shell-shocked. I was familiar with the condition. However, I never would've imagined that it would describe my own sister.

Since that day, I've watched my sister's slow and painful recovery from anorexia. It has been so hard for me to watch her make progress only to fear for her life when I see her backtrack. I've tried to find ways to encourage her, prayed for her daily, and praised God for her progress. One thing is for sure: recovery isn't easy, but it's so worth it—both for the individual with the eating disorder and for her family.

Acknowledgments

To my Savior, Jesus Christ: You deserve all of the honor and glory for my story—both for this book and for my recovery journey inside this book. You are the reason I was able to find real recovery. Thank You for never giving up on Your anorexia-prone child. You are my Healer, my Protector, my Provider, my Comforter, my Refuge, my Friend, and—most importantly—my Savior.

To my parents, Chris and Jennifer: Jesus has been using you in my life since before I was born. He knew that you could handle my craziness. Thank you for handling it well. Thank you for guiding me in the right direction, speaking the truth to me over and over, and supporting me as I share my story. Thank you for encouraging me to write and to keep writing. I love you both so much.

To my sisters, Anna and Jenna: You know me so well, and you always look out for me. You guys keep me straight, which is a blessing, even when I don't admit it in the moment. Y'all are the best besties that anyone could ever ask for, and I love y'all.

To my extended family members: I just want to say thank you for your prayers and your support over the years. Thank you for not bringing up my struggles when they were too painful for me to talk about, but thank you for praying me through the process. Love you all.

To my friends: I want you all to know that I'm grateful for your notes, emails, texts, and words of kindness. I've wanted to be a published author since I was a little girl, and your encouragement fueled me to pursue the publication of this book. Thank you.

To my counselors, Dr. Christine Buckingham, Mrs. Julia Flannagan, and Mrs. Rita Schulte: I know that we spent varying amounts of time together, but each of you was instrumental in helping me put anorexia behind me. You were patient when I was stubborn, and you were enthusiastic when I was weary. Thank you for your godly advice over the days, weeks, months, and years that we spent together. A lot of your advice is in this book! Keep doing what you're doing.

To my doctors and specialists, Dr. Charles Bennett, Mrs. Darleen Reinking, and Dr. Tomas Silber: you wanted to free me from Ed's grasp before I even knew that he was holding onto me. Jesus used your expertise, your prompting, and your objectivity in my life to help me recover. Thank you for putting up with my tears, my complaints, and my relapses.

About the Author

Grace McCready is a twenty-something who lives with her parents and two sisters. Although she doesn't enjoy drinking black coffee, running marathons, or reading books, she does enjoy spending time with her family, chatting with her friends, and watching her favorite TV shows. She graduated from Bryan College with a double major in business administration and communications. Her writing has been published across the web and in print. You can find more of her writing at her website, TizziesTidbitsofTruth.com.

For more information about
Grace McCready
and
Real Recovery
please visit:

www.TizziesTidbitsofTruth.com

Ambassador International's mission is to magnify the Lord Jesus Christ
and promote His Gospel through the written word.

We believe through the publication of Christian literature, Jesus Christ and
His Word will be exalted, believers will be strengthened in their walk with
Him, and the lost will be directed to Jesus Christ as the only way of salvation.

For more information about
AMBASSADOR INTERNATIONAL
please visit:

www.ambassador-international.com
@AmbassadorIntl
www.facebook.com/AmbassadorIntl

*Thank you for reading this book. Please consider leaving us a
review on your social media, favorite retailer's website,
Goodreads or Bookbub, or our website.*

More from Ambassador International

We live in an unpredictable, uncontrollable world where things change often, and fear can plant itself deeply within our hearts. **Chickening IN** is a practical approach to defeating the fear and doubt that is preventing us from becoming brave, bold women of God.

Although he holds a doctorate in depression, author Greg L. Russ chose to write this book from a patient's point of view. Having suffered five clinical bouts, Russ offers a graphic look inside the dark abyss while chronicling the insights he learned when his depression intersected God's mercy. The book extends an invitation to families, friends, churches and their pastors to become part of the comforting process.

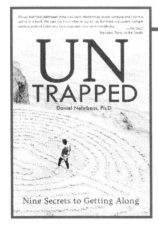

In *UnTrapped*, Dr. Nehrbass shows that whenever a relationship has you feeling trapped, you have options. While you may not be able to control another person's behavior, you can take control of your happiness by determining how you respond. Dr. Nehrbass shares real-life stories of people who've tried these options for relational change and he also offers biblical examples.

Made in the USA
Columbia, SC
11 April 2025

56493480R00065